# Social Studies Worksheets
# Don't Grow Dendrites

**20**
**Instructional Strategies That Engage the Brain**

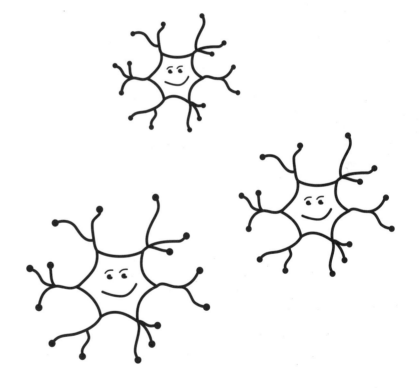

# Marcia L. Tate

**CORWIN**
A SAGE Company

CORWIN
A SAGE Company

FOR INFORMATION:

Corwin
A SAGE Company
2455 Teller Road
Thousand Oaks, California 91320
(800) 233-9936
Fax: (800) 417-2466
www.corwin.com

SAGE Publications Ltd.
1 Oliver's Yard
55 City Road
London EC1Y 1SP
United Kingdom

SAGE Publications India Pvt. Ltd.
B 1/I 1 Mohan Cooperative Industrial Area
Mathura Road, New Delhi 110 044
India

SAGE Publications Asia-Pacific Pte. Ltd.
33 Pekin Street #02-01
Far East Square
Singapore 048763

Acquisitions Editor:  Carol Chambers Collins
Associate Editor:  Megan Bedell
Editorial Assistant:  Sarah Bartlett
Project Editor:  Veronica Stapleton
Copy Editor:  Amy Rosenstein
Typesetter:  C&M Digitals (P) Ltd.
Proofreader:  Scott Oney
Indexer:  Sheila Bodell
Cover Designer:  Rose Storey
Permissions Editor:  Adele Hutchinson

Printed in the United States of America

*Library of Congress Cataloging-in-Publication Data*

Tate, Marcia L.

Social studies worksheets don't grow dendrites: 20 instructional
strategies that engage the brain/Marcia L. Tate.

p. cm.
Includes bibliographical references and index.

ISBN 978-1-4129-9875-8 (pbk. : acid-free paper)

1. Social sciences—Study and teaching (Elementary)—
United States. 2. Social sciences—Study and teaching (Middle
school)—United States. 3. Social sciences—Study and teaching
(Secondary)—United States. 4. Effective teaching. 5. Learning,
Psychology of. I. Title.

LB1584.T38 2012
372.83'044—dc23        2011040144

SUSTAINABLE FORESTRY INITIATIVE

Certified Chain of Custody
Promoting Sustainable Forestry
www.sfiprogram.org
SFI-01268

SFI label applies to text stock

11 12 13 14 15 10 9 8 7 6 5 4 3 2 1

# Contents

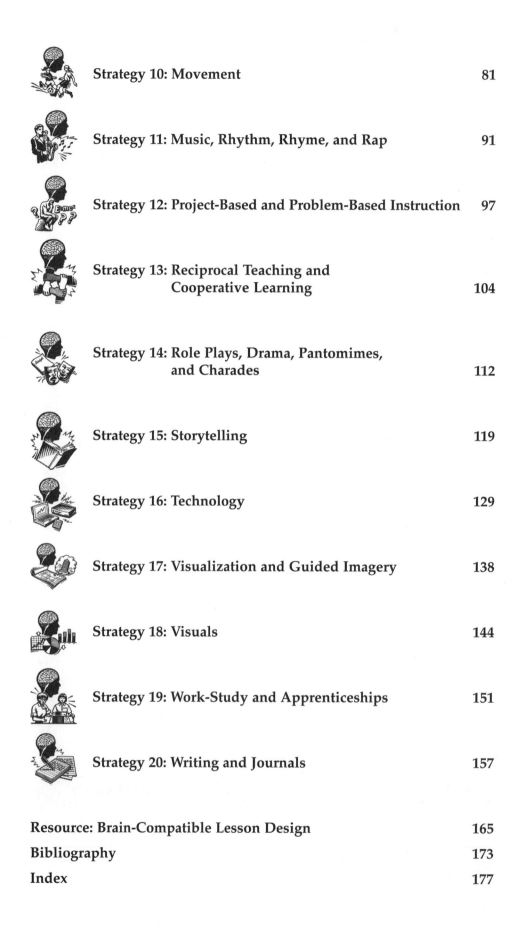

# Acknowledgments

S ocial studies was one of my least favorite subjects in school, even though I made great grades in my social studies classes. You see, I memorized a plethora of social studies facts needed to pass any test, but I only memorized those facts long enough to pass the tests. Because my long-term memory for social studies concepts is limited, this book has been challenging to write. Therefore, I am dedicating it to all of the teachers who make social studies their students' favorite subject, simply by the way they teach it. They tell stories, they engage students in role plays, they sing songs to help them remember, they provide students with real-life reasons to draw and write, or they help students visualize what life must have been like long ago and far away. In other words, they make social studies instruction relevant, interesting, and fun!

I also acknowledge the educational consultants, such as Eric Jensen, David Sousa, Robert Sylwester, and Patricia Wolfe, who continue to tell us how social studies, and every content area for that matter, should be taught. These are experts on the brain who continue to show us that *Worksheets Don't Grow Dendrites* and that concepts are long remembered if they are taught in ways that are compatible with how the brain actually acquires and retains information.

I owe a special debt of gratitude to the following two exemplary educators who made major content-specific contributions to this book: Debbie E. Daniell, K–12 Social Studies Director, Gwinnett County School System, Lawrenceville, Georgia, and Milissa Pfeiffer, Director of Social Studies K–12 for the Richardson Independent School District, Richardson, Texas. Special thanks to the social studies coordinators and teachers from around the country who provided me with additional information crucial to the writing of this book.

The continued support of my husband, Tyrone, and my children, Jennifer and her husband Lex, Jessica, and Christopher and his wife Amanda, enable me to write and consult with ease. I could not do it without their support!

I am especially grateful to our administrative assistant, Carol Purviance, and the team of associates who continue to make our company, *Developing Minds Inc.*, thrive. Thank you, Carol Collins, my editor, for your advice, support, and encouragement. You are truly appreciated!

## ■ PUBLISHER'S ACKNOWLEDGMENTS

Corwin gratefully acknowledges the contributions of the following reviewers:

Jeannie Benoit, Social Studies Teacher
Putnam Middle School, Putnam, Connecticut

Jane Carter Eason, Secondary Social Studies Consultant
Richland County School District One, Columbia, South Carolina

Dana Chibbaro, Director of Social Studies and Multicultural
Education
Newark Public Schools, Newark, New Jersey

Amy Davies, Social Studies Teacher
Taylor Allderdice High School, Pittsburgh, Pennsylvania

Kerry Dunne, K–12 Social Studies Director and Teaching American
History (TAH) Grant Program Director
Arlington Public Schools, Arlington, Massachusetts

Chris Elnicki, K–12 District Social Studies Coordinator and National
Social Studies Supervisor Association Board Member
Cherry Creek Schools, Centennial, Colorado

John P. Fry, Assistant Principal and Social Studies Curriculum
Committee Co-chair
Intermediate District 287, Plymouth, Minnesota

Cathy Hix, K–12 Social Studies Specialist and national trainer
Arlington Public Schools and The Teacher's Curriculum Institute,
Arlington, Virginia

# About the Author

**Marcia L. Tate, EdD,** is the former executive director of professional development for the DeKalb County School System, Decatur, Georgia. During her 30-year career with the district, she has been a classroom teacher, reading specialist, language arts coordinator, and staff development executive director. She received the Distinguished Staff Development Award for the State of Georgia, and her department was chosen to receive the Exemplary Program Award for the state.

Marcia is currently an educational consultant and has taught more than 350,000 administrators, teachers, parents, and business and community leaders throughout the world, including Australia, Egypt, Hungary, Singapore, Thailand, and New Zealand. She is the author of the following five best sellers: *Worksheets Don't Grow Dendrites: 20 Instructional Strategies That Engage the Brain; "Sit & Get" Won't Grow Dendrites: 20 Professional Learning Strategies That Engage the Adult Brain; Reading and Language Arts Worksheets Don't Grow Dendrites: 20 Literacy Strategies That Engage the Brain; Shouting Won't Grow Dendrites: 20 Techniques for Managing a Brain-Compatible Classroom; Mathematics Worksheets Don't Grow Dendrites: 20 Numeracy Strategies That Engage the Brain;* and the text *Science Worksheets Don't Grow Dendrites: 20 Instructional Strategies That Engage the Brain.* She is also the author of a popular book for parents called *Preparing Children for Success in School and in Life: 20 Ways to Increase Your Child's Brain Power.* Participants in her workshops refer to them as "some of the best ones they have ever experienced" since Marcia uses the 20 strategies outlined in her books to actively engage her audiences.

Marcia received her bachelor's degree in psychology and elementary education from Spelman College in Atlanta, Georgia. She earned her master's degree in remedial reading from the University of Michigan, her specialist degree in educational leadership from Georgia State University, and her doctorate in educational leadership from Clark Atlanta University. Spelman College awarded her the Apple Award for excellence in the field of education.

Marcia is married to Tyrone Tate and is the proud mother of three children: Jennifer, Jessica, and Christopher and the doting grandmother of two granddaughters, Christian and Aidan. Marcia can be contacted by calling her company at 770-918-5039 or by e-mail: marciata@bellsouth.net. Visit her Web site at www.developingmindsinc.com.

# Introduction

Visualize the two classrooms below and see if they remind you of any previous memories regarding the way in which you were taught social studies.

## SCENARIO I ▪

Michelle is a very conscientious student. It is very important to her that she make *As* in all of her classes. Today she enters her American history class at Lincoln Park High School. She takes her seat up front, which is where she chooses to sit in all of her classes. Michelle and the rest of the class are told to open their social studies textbooks and silently read Chapter 9, which contains *The Unanimous Declaration of the Thirteen United States of America,* while the teacher, Mrs. Simpson, is checking the roll. As soon as she is done, all students are told to be ready to read the chapter orally. Beginning with the student sitting in the first row, first desk students take turns orally reading *The Declaration of Independence.* Each student reads, some more fluently than others, until told to stop. Then the next one picks up where the last one left off. Since the teacher is calling on students in order, several students are counting down to the parts that they think will be theirs and are practicing. After all, no one purposely wants to sound bad when they read in front of the entire class.

When it is Michelle's turn, she reads perfectly, with expression; that is, as much expression as you can muster from a piece of expository text. Since most of the class is bored to tears, personal conversations sporadically break out from all over the room. Several students are text messaging while holding their cells phones out of the purview of the teacher, while others are scribbling on their paper. Class is so boring that they must find other ways to engage their brains!

The teacher then reads aloud to the class 30 slides from a PowerPoint presentation regarding the remainder of the first section in Chapter 9. When the PowerPoint is completed, students are asked to read the next section of the chapter silently for the rest of the period and answer the accompanying questions. It becomes obvious that most students do not take advantage of this option and choose instead to engage in alternate activities.

Chapter 9
The Declaration of Independence

# SCENARIO II ∎

Sarah is a student at Providence High School. Her American history class is her favorite since she is lucky enough to have a teacher, Mr. Martinez, who makes history *come alive* each day! Today's lesson is on *The Declaration of Independence*. As students file into class, they are greeted by their teacher, who is standing at the door while patriotic music is playing. By the way, no student is ever late for this class. They are too afraid that they will miss something important!

As they enter class, students know to look on the board for a meaningful activity that will either review content from the previous day or ready students for the lesson that is to follow. Today students have a choice to either individually draw or partner with another student to act out vocabulary words from yesterday's lesson. This activity consumes the first 15 minutes of the period but provides a much needed review of the content.

Mr. Martinez then reminds the class of their homework assignment, which was to read *The Unanimous Declaration of the Thirteen United States of America* from their textbook prior to coming to class. He opens the discussion by asking students how they typically spend their July 4 holiday each year and why we, as Americans, celebrate that date. He reminds them that the Declaration of Independence was adopted by Congress on July 4, 1776, making that date a special one for our country. He then randomly calls on students to stand and read selected sections of the document while he leads students in a thought-provoking discussion of its content.

Mr. Martinez asks students whether they have heard instances of teenagers asking the courts to be emancipated from their parents and all the ramifications that would entail. He asks them to consider the advantages and disadvantages of such a request. Following a spirited discussion, students are then requested to write their own personal *Declaration of Independence* from their parents, patterned after the one just discussed. Students spend time referring to the original document while crafting their personal declarations. Their documents should outline the grievances they have against their parents or guardians, just as the colonists did against the King of Great Britain in the original document. During the last part of the period, students volunteer to share their original *declarations* with the entire class. Then Mr. Martinez asks this question: *Would you like to present your parents with a copy of your declaration?* Most students agree that they would not! They concur that it would be too upsetting to their parents and that the emotional and financial support received from their parents would far outweigh the advantages of personal freedom at this stage in their lives.

# DÉJÀ VU ALL OVER AGAIN ■

What you probably do not realize is that Michelle is actually a description of me. My social studies classes were so boring but I considered myself a high achiever. I made straight *A*s in social studies classes in elementary and high school. (There was no such thing as middle school when I came along.) But I am not really bragging since, as an adult, I have very little memory of the content I was supposed to have learned.

Social Studies, to me, consisted of a large number of isolated names, facts, explorers, and so forth, which I memorized. Here was the problem. I memorized them only long enough to pass the numerous tests I was given. That is how I made the *A*s. Unfortunately, once the tests were over, so was the information. As an adult, I have come to realize that one can make straight *A*s in their classes and not have truly learned much of anything. All you have to have is a fairly good memory for a short period of time.

Social studies is one of the easiest content areas for teachers to be tempted to use lecture and worksheets to have students cover content and cram for exams. But, like a famous educator, Madeline Hunter, once said, *If all you are doing is covering content, then take a shovel and cover it with dirt, since it is dead to memory!*

If you are having students attempt to recall information that you believe they need to know, you are fighting a losing battle. I have learned that between the years 4 B.C. and A.D. 1900, information doubled. Information doubled again between 1900 and 1964. In other words, what initially took more than 1,900 years to accomplish only took 64 years the second time around. Now, depending on which source you read, with the invention of the Internet, information is doubling every 12 to 24 months. Therefore, there is no way that a student can hold in short- or long-term memory all of the things they need to know and understand. Nor should they! Isn't it more important that students comprehend certain major concepts in social studies and then know how to locate any additional information essential for answering a question, dealing with an issue, or solving a problem?

Here is a true story that illustrates the point I am making. I was asked to teach a social studies lesson in a middle school not too long ago. Whenever I come in to conduct a model lesson with students, I always ask the teacher ahead of time what he or she would like me to teach. In other words, what is the objective of the lesson and what should students know or be able to do by the time the lesson is completed? I was told that students needed to learn and remember the original 13 colonies in the United States, who founded each colony, and the year in which it was founded. Although I can understand why students need to know the names of the original colonies, I do not know why it is important that they memorize the year in which each separate colony was founded. That information can be easily located on a need-to-know basis. Class time would have been better spent examining the reasons for which the colonies were founded and how the climate and topography of each colony contributed to its economy. Therefore, that is exactly what I taught!

# ■  THE THEMES OF SOCIAL STUDIES

Before we look at how to teach social studies, let's consider what major concepts should be taught. According to the *National Curriculum Standards for Social Studies: A Framework for Teaching, Learning, and Assessment* (2010), published by the National Council for the Social Studies, the following 10 major themes should be an integral part of any social studies curriculum. The paragraphs that follow delineate the 10 themes and provide a brief description of each theme. Notice how the content of the themes overlaps since no one theme is an entity unto itself.

## Culture

*Social studies programs should include experiences
that provide for the study of culture and cultural diversity.*

When students study the theme of culture, they learn about the values, beliefs, behaviors, institutions, and traditions of a group of people by examining their language, music, arts, literature, and artifacts. They realize that there are similarities and differences in cultures but that they are dynamic and, therefore, change over time. In the early grades, students begin to explore the likenesses and differences of cultures and to recognize the cultural basis for some ways of life in their communities as well as throughout the world. By the middle grades, students are looking more in-depth at various aspects of culture such as beliefs and language and how time and place influence cultural development. High school students are drawing from other disciplines in an effort to comprehend more difficult cultural concepts such as assimilation, adaptation, acculturation, and dissonance.

## Time, Continuity, and Change

*Social studies programs should include experiences
that provide for the study of the past and its legacy.*

During this theme, students realize that by analyzing the history of a group of people's values, ideals, and traditions, they can discern patterns of continuity and change over time. In the early grades, children experience how the stories of the past can be told differently and why they differ. They begin to comprehend the relationship between the decisions humans make and the consequences of those decisions. By the middle grades, students delve more deeply into an appreciation for various perspectives on history, realizing that those perspectives are influenced by cultural traditions, values of society, the sources one selects, and their individual experiences. By high school, students are making more informed decisions by locating and analyzing multiple sources and discerning the differences in the accounts of others.

## People, Places, and Environments

*Social studies programs should include experiences*
*that provide for the study of people, places, and environments.*

When students study this theme, they learn where people live and why they decide to live there. They explore physical systems such as weather and seasons, natural resources, and the impact of climate on human populations. Students identify the important economic, social, and cultural characteristics of different people in various locations. In the early grades, students are more focused on their personal neighborhoods, cities, and states but are able to use maps, globes, and other tools to study distant people and places. By the middle grades, students are looking at issues impacting people and places in this country and throughout the world, with particular attention to concepts such as migration and changes in the global environment. High school students become capable of evaluating and recommending public policy based on their knowledge of complex processes of change in the relationships between people and their environments.

## Individual Development and Identity

*Social studies programs should include experiences that provide for*
*the study of individual development and identity.*

Drawing from the fields of psychology, anthropology, and sociology, this theme enables students to answer such questions as *How do we interact with other people culturally, socially, and politically in ways that enable us to develop into the individuals that we become?* Students will examine their personal skill level in working toward individual goals while attempting to understand the feelings and beliefs of others as well. In the early grades, students concentrate on their personal identities within the context of their own families, peers, and communities. By the middle grades, students are looking at themselves in light of their relationship to other people and examining individual differences in various cultures and societies. By high school, students are applying concepts from fields such as psychology and sociology to look at patterns of human behavior across cultures.

## Individuals, Groups, and Institutions

*Social studies programs should include experiences that provide for*
*the study of interactions among individuals, groups, and institutions.*

When studying this theme, students learn how such institutions as families, schools, religious institutions, courts, and government agencies are formed, influenced, maintained, and changed as well as how they influence people and the culture. In the early grades, students study a variety of institutions that affect them personally and how those institutions change as individuals and groups change. They also study how groups can come into conflict with one another. By the middle grades, students are learning how to use institutions to work for the common good. High school students are examining traditions that serve as the foundation for political and social institutions as well as how those institutions reflect the beliefs, needs, and interests of people.

## Power, Authority, and Governance

*Social studies programs should include experiences that provide for the study of how people create, interact with, and change structures of power, authority, and governance.*

By studying the basic values and ideals of a democracy, as well as other governmental systems during this theme, students learn how nations establish their security and order and how they resolve conflict. They study the purpose of government, its proper scope and limits, and how individual rights are affected within the context of a system where the majority rules. Students in the early grades are considering what constitutes fairness and order in different contexts. During the middle grades, students examine a variety of century-old systems that have given people power and authority to govern. High school students are looking more closely at more abstract principles of governance. However, all students should be provided with real-life opportunities to participate in different levels of power, authority, and governance at the classroom, local, state, and national levels.

## Production, Distribution, and Consumption

*Social studies programs should include experiences that provide for the study of how people organize for the production, distribution, and consumption of goods and services.*

Since resources are unequally distributed, students explore the fact that systems of exchange must exist. While studying this theme, they learn that economic decisions are becoming increasingly global and the world more interdependent. Students will pair their critical thinking skills with data to decide how to deal with the real-life issue of scarcity of resources. In the early grades, students begin to consider their wants versus needs as they compare their own personal experiences with those of other people. They also examine the consequences of personal economic decisions on the larger community, the nation, and the world. Middle grade students take what they have learned to address answers to basic questions of economics. By high school, this theme is emphasizing domestic and global economic policies as they relate to such issues as trade, unemployment, health care, and the use of resources.

## Science, Technology, and Society

*Social studies programs should include experiences that
provide for the study of relationships among
science, technology, and society.*

Modern life is dependent on technology, but do new technologies actually improve the society for which they were created? Is technology use out of control, and can society preserve its values and beliefs in a technology-linked world? How can the greatest number of people in society benefit from technology? These are just a few of the questions addressed as students study this theme. Students in the early grades examine the history of technology and how inventions like the wheel, automobiles, transistor radios, airplanes, and air conditioning influenced the human values and behaviors of their time. By the middle grades, students are considering whether technology is beginning to control us or we it. High school students examine real-life controversial issues such as genetic engineering, electronic surveillance, and medical technology.

## Global Connections

*Social studies programs should include experiences that
provide for the study of global connections and interdependence.*

To understand global interdependence, students must realize the important connections among societies throughout the world. While studying this theme, students analyze the conflict that can exist between national and global interests and priorities and examine possible solutions in critical fields such as human rights, the quality of the environment, health care, and economic development. Students in the early grades learn to derive action plans that address basic global issues and concerns. By the middle years, students can analyze how states and nations interact and how they respond to global change. By high school, students are reflecting on personal, national, and global decisions regarding critical issues such as human rights, universal peace, trade, and ecology.

## Civic Ideals and Practices

*Social studies programs should include experiences that
provide for the study of the ideals, principles, and
practices of citizenship in a democratic republic.*

The central purpose of social studies is to provide students with an understanding of the civic ideals and practices necessary for becoming a fully participating member of a democratic society. This theme attempts to do just that. Students learn about their basic freedoms and rights and the practices and institutions that support them. Students in the early grades accomplish this by setting classroom rules and expectations, creating mock elections, and using the strategies of storytelling and role play to experience civic ideals in other places and times. Middle school students should be capable of visualizing themselves in civic roles within their own communities, but by high school, they should be identifying needs in society, determining public policy, and working for the dignity of the individual as well as for the good of society as a whole.

# ■ BRAIN-COMPATIBLE SOCIAL STUDIES INSTRUCTION

Now that we know what should be taught, let's examine how we should teach it. Teachers should be experts on the brain. After all, they are teaching brains every day. In fact, every time a student learns something new, his brain grows a new brain cell, called a *dendrite*. Therefore, teachers should actually be classified as *dendrite* growers! What I find, however, is that many teachers know very little about the vessel that they are expecting to hold vast amounts of information, particularly in the content area of social studies.

Learning-style theorists (Dewey, 1934, 1938; Gardner, 1983; Marzano, 2007; Sternberg & Grigorenko, 2000) and educational consultants (Caine, Caine, McClintic, & Klimek, 2009; Jensen, 2002, 2008; Sousa, 2006, 2011) who research the brain have all concluded that there are certain instructional strategies that, by their very nature, result in long-term retention. These strategies are not new. Most have been used by memorable teachers for generations. What is new is that the brain research is providing some insight as to why these strategies work better than others, such as lecture or worksheets. I call these strategies brain-compatible since they take advantage of the way the brain learns best, and I have synthesized them into 20 ways to deliver instruction.

The 20 strategies are as follows:

1. Brainstorming and discussion

2. Drawing and artwork

3. Field trips

4. Games

5. Graphic organizers, semantic maps, and word webs

6. Humor

7. Manipulatives, experiments, labs, and models

8. Metaphors, analogies, and similes

9. Mnemonic devices

10. Movement

11. Music, rhythm, rhyme, and rap

12. Project-based and problem-based instruction

13. Reciprocal teaching and cooperative learning

14. Role plays, drama, pantomimes, and charades

15. Storytelling

16. Technology

17. Visualization and guided imagery

18. Visuals

19. Work-study and apprenticeships

20. Writing and journals

Refer to Figure 0.1 for a correlation of the 20 brain-compatible strategies to Howard Gardner's Theory of Multiple Intelligences and to the four major modalities—(1) visual, (2) auditory, (3) kinesthetic, and (4) tactile.

These strategies not only increase academic achievement for all students, since they address every single intelligence and modality and decrease behavior problems as well as actively engage every brain and reduce boredom, but they also make teaching and learning so much fun!

## OVERVIEW OF THE BOOK ∎

This social studies book will complete the set of multiple content-area books in the series about *growing dendrites.* The additional books are as follows:

- *Worksheets Don't Grow Dendrites: 20 Instructional Strategies That Engage the Brain*

- *Reading and Language Arts Worksheets Don't Grow Dendrites: 20 Literacy Strategies That Engage the Brain*

- *Mathematics Worksheets Don't Grow Dendrites: 20 Numeracy Strategies That Engage the Brain PreK–8*

- *Science Worksheets Don't Grow Dendrites: 20 Instructional Strategies That Engage the Brain*

This book, like the others in the series, attempts to accomplish the following four major objectives:

1. Review the research regarding the 20 brain-compatible strategies and why they provide best practices for teaching and learning;

2. Supply more than 200 classroom examples of the application of the 20 strategies for teaching the 10 themes of social studies;

3. Provide time and space at the end of each chapter for the reader to reflect on the application of these strategies as they apply to the social studies curriculum; and

4. Demonstrate how to plan and deliver unforgettable social studies lessons by asking the five questions on the lesson plan format in the Resource section of this book.

This is one of the easiest books to read that you will ever add to your professional library. There are 20 chapters, one for each strategy. The chapters do not even have to be read sequentially. If you wish to read about the impact of *Movement* for teaching social studies, then start reading at Chapter 10. The sample activities in each chapter are correlated to a specific grade range and one or more social studies themes. But the sample activities are just that—samples. They are intended to provide you with examples of how you can integrate the strategies into your social studies lessons and are not meant to be an exhaustive list. Once you start thinking, you will be able to generate a plethora of additional activities for each strategy.

If you really think about the list of 20, these strategies are used most often in the primary grades. What we know now is that these strategies work for all students, regardless of age, ability level, grade level, or content area. In fact, when these strategies begin to be used less by teachers is precisely when students' grades, academic achievement, confidence, and love of school also decrease. The advantage to having activities ranging from early grades through high school in the same book is that the reader can easily select activities that will meet the needs of students performing below, on, and above grade level. This will enable you to more easily differentiate instruction. You will also find that an activity designed for a specific grade range can be taken as is or easily adapted for another grade range.

The reflection page at the end of each chapter enables the reader to think about ways in which they are already incorporating the strategy as well as new activities they would choose to create.

The lesson planning section asks five questions that help the reader synthesize the process of planning an unforgettable lesson.

In conclusion, consider the following riddle:

> *What is the difference between a person who*
> *crams for a social studies exam and makes an* A *and a person*
> *who crams for the exam and makes an* F?

Give up! The answer is simple. The person who crams for the exam and makes an *A* remembers the information until 10 minutes *after* the test. The person who crams for the exam and makes an *F* remembers the information until 10 minutes *before* the test.

If you will teach the 10 social studies themes using the 20 brain-compatible strategies outlined in the chapters that follow, not only will your students remember the information long after the test is over, but their grades will be better than ever, their achievement scores higher than you thought possible, the content itself more relevant, and teaching social studies will become a blast! As a side benefit, you will become their favorite teacher if you are not already!

| Comparison of Brain-Compatible Instructional Strategies to Learning Theory | | |
|---|---|---|
| *Brain-Compatible Strategies* | *Multiple Intelligences* | *Visual, Auditory, Kinesthetic, Tactile (VAKT)* |
| Brainstorming and discussion | Verbal-linguistic | Auditory |
| Drawing and artwork | Spatial | Kinesthetic/tactile |
| Field trips | Naturalist | Kinesthetic/tactile |
| Games | Interpersonal | Kinesthetic/tactile |
| Graphic organizers, semantic maps, and word webs | Logical-mathematical/ spatial | Visual/tactile |
| Humor | Verbal-linguistic | Auditory |
| Manipulatives, experiments, labs, and models | Logical-mathematical | Tactile |
| Metaphors, analogies, and similes | Spatial | Visual/auditory |
| Mnemonic devices | Musical-rhythmic | Visual/auditory |
| Movement | Bodily-kinesthetic | Kinesthetic |
| Music, rhythm, rhyme, and rap | Musical-rhythmic | Auditory |
| Project-based and problem-based learning | Logical-mathematical | Visual/tactile |
| Reciprocal teaching and cooperative learning | Verbal-linguistic | Auditory |
| Role plays, drama, pantomimes, and charades | Bodily-kinesthetic | Kinesthetic |
| Storytelling | Verbal-linguistic | Auditory |
| Technology | Spatial | Visual/tactile |
| Visualization and guided imagery | Spatial | Visual |
| Visuals | Spatial | Visual |
| Work-study and apprenticeships | Interpersonal | Kinesthetic |
| Writing and journals | Intrapersonal | Visual/tactile |

Figure 0.1

# Strategy 1

# Brainstorming and Discussion

## WHAT: DEFINING THE STRATEGY

*How am I different from and similar to others?*

*In what ways can cultures be compared, and what can we learn from comparisons?*

*How have national and global regions developed and changed over time?*

*What events and turning points are important in history and why?*

*What are key democratic ideals and practices?*

*How do individuals, groups, and institutions deal with market failures?*

—National Council for the Social Studies, 2010

It has been said that the two things that the brain needs most in order to learn are the two things that students cannot do in many classrooms—students cannot talk and they cannot move. One teacher shared in a workshop that we, as parents, spend the first 3 years of our children's lives teaching them to walk and talk and the next 15 years telling them to *sit down and shut up!* Why not use the brain's natural inclination to talk with peers to engage students in brainstorming and discussion activities. Students are going to talk anyway and most of the time it should be about the content. After all, the person doing the most talking about the content is growing the most dendrites (brain cells)! In many classrooms, that is the teacher. We have many brilliant teachers in the business. What we need is an abundance of brilliant students!

Why not engage students in meaningful discussion regarding social studies using open-ended questions similar to the ones listed above? Just remember to use the following *DOVE* guidelines:

- **D**efer judgment: Have students discuss or brainstorm as many ideas as possible in a designated amount of time. Students should not comment either positively or negatively about another student's ideas.
- **O**ne idea at a time: Each time an idea is presented, it should be written down, and every student should give his or her full attention to that one idea.
- **V**ariety of ideas: Students should be encouraged to share as many ideas as possible and to *think outside the box*.
- **E**nergy on task: All students should focus on the task and not be distracted by any other diversion.

The strategy of brainstorming and discussion can be used with the whole class, or students can be placed in cooperative groups of four to six students and the activity replicated in each group. If students work in small groups, a whole-class discussion should follow where groups report their results.

---

# WHY: THEORETICAL FRAMEWORK

When students are taught to investigate and form opinions regarding a topic so that they can defend their beliefs and ideas, they are establishing a pluralist approach to content (Melber & Hunter, 2010).

Being allowed to dialogue with others who have different perspectives is a civic engagement strategy that helps students prepare for becoming responsible and competent citizens (National Council for the Social Studies, 2010).

Not allowing for any discussion during class time is one of the top 14 stress producers in adolescent brains (Feinstein, 2009).

Following an actual experience, having students verbally retell events and ideas through discussion and dialogue assists the brain in tapping into cognitive memory (Fogarty, 2009).

Discussion enhances the learning experience for students who have visual processing problems (Green & Casale-Giannola, 2011).

When a teacher asks open-ended questions, the minds of all levels of readers are stimulated and critical thinking and lifelong reading and writing skills are encouraged (Algozzine, Campbell, & Wang, 2009a).

Questions during brainstorming and discussion should be divided into two general categories: (1) those that can be answered by deductive

> reasoning or where one can find the correct answer to the question by deducing it from the data provided, and (2) those that can be answered by inductive reasoning or questions where there may be multiple solutions to one problem (Delandtsheer, 2011).
>
> The purpose of discussion is to talk about something in a friendly and constructive manner while offering data, ideas, knowledge, information, and rationales for opinions and positions and attempting to convince others to accept a particular position (Costa, 2008).
>
> Current research suggests that the real learning that a social scientist undertakes is not founded on answers but questions (Harada & Kim, 2003).
>
> The process of discussion and debate supports students as they develop their ability to think critically (Wolf, 2003).

# HOW: INSTRUCTIONAL ACTIVITIES

**WHO:**      Early Grades

**WHEN:**      Before or during a lesson

**THEME(S):**      Power, Authority, and Governance

- At the beginning of the school year, explain to students how the classroom requires basic rules and routines to maintain order and keep students both physically and psychologically safe. Have them work together as a class to brainstorm a list of rules, routines, and procedures for the classroom. Have the class reach a consensus on which rules they will accept. Then discuss how these same concepts apply to the larger society.

**WHO:**      Early and Middle Grades, High School

**WHEN:**      Before a lesson

**THEME(S):**      All

- The social studies textbook can be difficult to comprehend for some students. Make it easier for all students by having them peruse captions, pictures, charts, graphs, bold headings, and so forth prior to reading the text to determine what the chapter will be about. Following the chapter survey, have students brainstorm a list of questions that they wish to answer connected to the text. Then, have them read the chapter in small sections for the purpose of answering the questions that they themselves generated (Tate, 2010).

**WHO:**      Early and Middle Grades, High School

**WHEN:**      During a lesson

**THEME(S):**      All

- When asking questions in class or creating teacher-made tests, provide opportunities for all students to be successful by asking both knowledge questions and those that enable students to use their higher level thinking skills. Refer to Bloom's Taxonomy Revised (Figure 1.1) to ensure that students have opportunities to answer questions at all levels of the revised taxonomy, particularly those above the *knowledge* level (Tate, 2010).

**WHO:**         Early and Middle Grades, High School

**WHEN:**        During a lesson

**THEME(S):**    All

- Teach students the difference between *minnow* or *skinny* questions and *whale* or *fat* questions. Skinny questions are those that call for immediate recall of facts and may have their place at times. However, whale questions are higher level ones and call for students to explain, analyze, or predict based on knowledge that has been previously attained. The question stems found in the Bloom's Taxonomy chart from the preceding activity can be referred to when formulating minnow and whale questions regarding a social studies topic for discussion (Berman, 2008, p. 10).

**WHO:**         Early and Middle Grades, High School

**WHEN:**        During a lesson

**THEME(S):**    Production, Distribution, and Consumption

- Engage students in a whole-class discussion regarding production, distribution, and consumption of goods and services by asking age-appropriate questions such as the following:
  - Why can't people have all that they want of everything?
  - What is the difference between needs and wants?
  - How do people make decisions about what goods are produced and how to distribute them?
  - How do governments make economic decisions?
  - How do different types of economic systems function?
  - How do governments use fiscal and monetary policy to influence the economy or to affect households and businesses?

**WHO:**         Early and Middle Grades, High School

**WHEN:**        During a lesson

**THEME(S):**    All

- Present a controversial issue to the class, such as, *In light of the impact of the tsunami on the nuclear reactors following the Japanese earthquake, is nuclear energy worth the risks?* or, *Debate the internment of Japanese Americans during World War II.* Divide the class in half and have them research and prepare a debate for one side of the issue or the other. Then, have some students role play the debate as they take turns serving on opposing teams and presenting their arguments to the class. Have students prepare a rubric that will delineate how the debate is to be judged. Then, you be the judge or have another teacher judge which side presented a more convincing argument while adhering to the rubric (Tate, 2010).

**WHO:**          Middle Grades, High School

**WHEN:**        During a lesson

**THEME(S):**    Power, Authority, and Governance

- Divide students into groups of four to six. Have each group conduct research on one of the following topics: (1) How do governments (unitary, confederation, and federal) distribute power? (2) How do citizens participate in autocratic, oligarchic, and democratic forms of government? (3) What are the characteristics of parliamentary and presidential forms of democratic governments? Have students record their information in a graphic organizer, which will enable them to debate the pros and cons of each form of government.

**WHO:**          Middle Grades, High School

**WHEN:**        During a lesson

**THEME(S):**    Individual Development and Identity

- Engage students in a whole-class discussion on the impact of stereotyping and bias as well as conformity in the middle or high school setting and their personal reaction to those terms. Have them volunteer to share stories of times when they personally experienced these concepts. Extend the discussion to the impact of stereotyping, bias, and conformity on the larger society as a whole.

**WHO:**          Middle Grades, High School

**WHEN:**        During a lesson

**THEME(S):**    Global Connections

- Engage students in a whole-class discussion regarding what rights are considered fundamental for all human beings regardless of the part of the world in which they live.

**WHO:**          High School

**WHEN:**        During a lesson

**THEME(S):**    All

- Assist students in identifying some real-world problems such as rising gas prices, the economic downturn in the United States, or changing climate conditions. Have students brainstorm possible solutions to the problems and the implications of the solutions for individuals, groups, or institutions (National Council for the Social Studies, 2010).

## Bloom's Taxonomy Revised

Bloom's Taxonomy (1956) has stood the test of time. Recently, Anderson and Krathwohl (2001) have proposed some minor changes to include the renaming and reordering of the taxonomy. This reference reflects those recommended changes.

### I. REMEMBER (KNOWLEDGE)
**(shallow processing: drawing out factual answers, testing recall, and recognition)**

| *Verbs for Objectives* | *Model Questions* | *Instructional Strategies* |
|---|---|---|
| Choose | Who? | Highlighting |
| Describe | Where? | Rehearsal |
| Define | Which one? | Memorizing |
| Identify | What? | Mnemonics |
| Label | How? | |
| List | What is the best one? | |
| Locate | Why? | |
| Match | How much? | |
| Memorize | When? | |
| Name | What does it mean? | |
| Omit | | |
| Recite | | |
| Recognize | | |
| Select | | |
| State | | |

### II. UNDERSTAND (COMPREHENSION)
**(translating, interpreting, and extrapolating)**

| *Verbs for Objectives* | *Model Questions* | *Instructional Strategies* |
|---|---|---|
| Classify | State in your own words. | Key examples |
| Defend | What does this mean? | Emphasize connections |
| Demonstrate | Give an example. | Elaborate concepts |
| Distinguish | Condense this paragraph. | Summarize |
| Explain | State in one word . . . | Paraphrase |
| Express | What part doesn't fit? | STUDENTS explain |
| Extend | What exceptions are there? | STUDENTS state the rule |
| Give Example | What are they saying? | "Why does this example . . . ?" |
| Illustrate | What seems to be . . . ? | create visual representation |
| Indicate | Which are facts? | (concept maps, outlines, flow |
| Interrelate | Is this the same as . . . ? | charts, organizers, analogies, pro/con grids) PRO/CON |
| Interpret | Read the graph (table). | Note: The faculty member can show them, but they have to do it. |
| Infer | Select the best definition. | Metaphors, rubrics, heuristics |
| Judge | What would happen if . . . ? | |
| Match | Explain what is happening. | |
| Paraphrase | Explain what is meant. | |
| Represent | What seems likely? | |
| Restate | This represents . . . | |
| Rewrite | Is it valid that . . . ? | |
| Select | Which statement supports . . . ? | |

*(Continued)*

**Figure 1.1** (Continued)

| Show | What restrictions would you add? |
| Summarize | Show in a graph or table. |
| Tell | |
| Translate | |

---

## III. APPLY

**(knowing when to apply; why to apply; and recognizing patterns of transfer to situations that are new or unfamiliar or that have a new slant for students)**

| Verbs for Objectives | Model Questions | Instructional Strategies |
| --- | --- | --- |
| Apply | Predict what would happen if . . . | Modeling |
| Choose | Choose the best statements that apply. | Cognitive apprenticeships |
| Dramatize | Judge the effects. | "Mindful" practice—NOT just a |
| Explain | What would result. | "routine practice" |
| Generalize | Tell what would happen. | Part and whole sequencing |
| Judge | Tell how, when, where, why. | Authentic situations |
| Organize | Tell how much change there would be. | "Coached" practice |
| Paint | Identify the results of . . . | Case studies |
| Prepare | | Simulations |
| Produce | | Algorithms |
| Select | | |
| Show | | |
| Sketch | | |
| Solve | | |
| Use | | |

---

## IV. ANALYZE (breaking down into parts, forms)

| Verbs for Objectives | Model Questions | Instructional Strategies |
| --- | --- | --- |
| Analyze | What is the function of . . . ? | Models of thinking |
| Categorize | What's fact? Opinion? | Challenging assumptions |
| Classify | What assumptions? | Retrospective analysis |
| Compare | What statement is relevant? | Reflection through journaling |
| Differentiate | What motive is there? | Debates |
| Distinguish | Related to, extraneous to, not applicable. | Discussions and other collaborating learning activities |
| Identify | What conclusions? | Decision-making situations |
| Infer | What does the author believe? | |
| Point Out | What does the author assume? | |
| Select | Make a distinction. | |
| Subdivide | State the point of view of . . . | |
| Survey | What is the premise? | |
| | What ideas apply? | |
| | What ideas justify the conclusion? | |
| | What's the relationship between? | |

The least essential statements
are
What's the main idea? Theme?
What inconsistencies, fallacies?
What literary form is used?
What persuasive technique?
Implicit in the statement is . . .

## V. EVALUATE (according to some set of criteria, and state why)

| Verbs for Objectives | Model Questions | Instructional Strategies |
|---|---|---|
| Appraise | What fallacies, consistencies, or inconsistencies appear? | Challenging assumptions |
| Judge | | Journaling |
| Criticize | Which is more important, moral, better, logical, valid, appropriate? | Debates |
| Defend | Find the errors. | Discussions and other collaborating learning activities |
| Compare | | Decision-making situations |

## VI. CREATE (SYNTHESIS)
**(combining elements into a pattern not clearly there before)**

| Verbs for Objectives | Model Questions | Instructional Strategies |
|---|---|---|
| Choose | How would you test . . . ? | Modeling |
| Combine | Propose an alternative. | Challenging assumptions |
| Compose | Solve the following. | Reflection through journaling |
| Construct | How else would you . . . ? | Debates |
| Create | State a rule. | Discussions and other |
| Design | | collaborating learning activities |
| Develop | | Design |
| Do | | Decision-making situations |
| Formulate | | |
| Hypothesize | | |
| Invent | | |
| Make | | |
| Make Up | | |
| Originate | | |
| Organize | | |
| Plan | | |
| Produce | | |
| Role Play | | |
| Tell | | |

**Figure 1.1**   Key Words, Model Questions, and Instruction Strategies

Compiled by the IUPUI Center for Teaching and Learning. Revised December 2002.

# REFLECTION AND APPLICATION

How will I incorporate *brainstorming and discussion*
into instruction to engage students' brains?

**Which brainstorming and discussion activities am I already
incorporating into my social studies curriculum?**

**What additional brainstorming and discussion activities will
I incorporate?**

# Strategy 2

# Drawing and Artwork

## WHAT: DEFINING THE STRATEGY

Students in Linda Field's high school class were asked to outline the chapter on South Asia. This chapter delineated the climate, geography, natural resources, and so forth, of the continent. After Linda came to my *Worksheets Don't Grow Dendrites* workshop, she began using the strategy of drawing to her advantage. She started giving students the option of outlining the chapters in a linear fashion with Roman numerals and alphabets or of drawing out the most important concepts in the chapter. Several of her students choose the drawing option, including John. When Linda came to a subsequent workshop, she bought one of John's drawings that I now show to teachers as an example of how a student's gift of drawing can be used to support content. She related to me that John's grades in social studies improved almost immediately and his picture showed that he is truly a talented artist. However, more important than that is his ability to know more social studies as he processes the subject through his artwork.

If teachers would just allow students to use drawing as one of many strategies for teaching content, more students, like John, would be successful. In every book I have written, I relate the story of my son, Chris, who also draws beautifully, but had only one teacher in high school who enabled him and other students to use their talents in class. As I write this book, Chris is enrolled in the Atlanta Art Institute where he is getting a Bachelor's degree in Media Arts and Animation, and the products and projects he is producing are wonderful! Will there be jobs for Chris and John in the real world? Absolutely! Why not use the real-world talent with which they were born to teach the content in school that they need to know. The activities in this chapter will provide activities for incorporating drawing and artwork into the teaching of social studies content.

---

## WHY: THEORETICAL FRAMEWORK

Drawing an image or nonlinguistic representation is a broad-based literacy strategy that can help students comprehend written sources during instruction (National Council for the Social Studies, 2010).

Learning opportunities that incorporate the arts enable all students, with or without a disability, to experience success, use all of their senses, and show their intelligence (Algozzine, Campbell, & Wang, 2009a).

Artwork can be used by social studies teachers to provide many different perspectives about past events and the people who lived them (Melber & Hunter, 2010).

Art is a means by which students can express themselves while enhancing their understanding of the curriculum and releasing stress, emotions, and pent-up energy (Karten, 2009).

The shared emotion between the painter and those who see the work of art not only assists in maintaining important cognitive systems; it also increases the awareness and development of social skills (Sylwester, 2010).

Social studies teachers can join with art teachers to create interdisciplinary units that are centered on topics in social studies (Gullatt, 2008).

When students draw or add doodles to their notes, they create visuals that help them understand, process, or encode information and recall new information as well (Allen, 2008a).

Art increases curricular insights for students who respond well when visuals go along with or explain more complicated vocabulary or concepts in history or other disciplines (Karten, 2009).

Drawing pictures and pictographs is one activity that aids students in the nonlinguistic (or mental) processing of information (Marzano, 2007).

Paintings not only depict the artist's interpretation of the subject; they can also tell a great deal about the place and time when the art was actually created (Janson & Janson, 2003).

Thinking in other curricular areas is preceded by thinking in art (Dewey, 1934).

# HOW: INSTRUCTIONAL ACTIVITIES

**WHO:**          Early Grades

**WHEN:**          Before, during, or after a lesson

**THEME(S):**     Individual Development and Identity

- Have students draw two pictures of themselves, one near the beginning of the school year and one closer to the middle or end of the school year. Students should be prepared to explain how they have personally changed during the course of the year. Engage students in a whole-class discussion of how individuals' looks, abilities, interests, and talents change over time.

**WHO:**          Early Grades

**WHEN:**          After a lesson

**THEME(S):**     People, Places, and Environments

- To help students comprehend locations of people and their environments, draw a map of the classroom on the board as a visual. Place important things from the classroom on the map. Once students understand the concept, expand their understanding to a map of the school and then of their community. For homework, have students draw a map of the route from their house or apartment to the school. Have students label street names and places of importance to them on their maps. Then have the students show their maps and explain them to the class.

**WHO:**          Early Grades

**WHEN:**          During a lesson

**THEME(S):**     Individuals, Groups, and Institutions

- Have a discussion with students on the work roles that people fill in the school and their community. Following the discussion, have each student draw one role or find a picture of a person fulfilling that role from a magazine or other source. Put all of the students' pictures together in a collage to post in the room as a visual. Broaden students' horizons by introducing them to additional work roles that may not be reflected in their respective communities but to which they might aspire one day.

**WHO:**          Early and Middle Grades, High School

**WHEN:**          During or after a lesson

**THEME(S):**     All

- Have students create a personal *Pictionary* by illustrating assigned social studies vocabulary words. Each page of the *Pictionary* consists of an assigned word written in a color of choice, a drawing that illustrates the meaning of the word, and an original sentence that uses the word in the appropriate context. Some words are easier to illustrate than others. For example, *migration* or *immigration* would be relatively easy while the term *democracy* might not be. However, that is where the creativity of students comes in. To illustrate *democracy* students could draw a picture of citizens voting for one candidate from among many candidates.

**WHO:**          Early and Middle Grades, High School

**WHEN:**         During a lesson

**THEME(S):**     Culture

- Have students select a particular culture or social group and make a collage, either by drawing or by collecting pictures, of the commonly held values, beliefs, traditions, and behaviors that are characteristic of that culture. As students display their collages, assist them in making comparisons between cultures and determine similarities and differences.

**WHO:**          Early and Middle Grades, High School

**WHEN:**         After a lesson

**THEME(S):**     All

- Place paper that you would use for a bulletin board across one wall in your classroom. When students enter the room, give each one a marker and a spot on the paper. The class assignment is to design a class mural that would delineate what the class recalls regarding a chapter or unit of study. Each student draws only one specific thing that he or she remembers and must be able to discuss with the class what was drawn and why. Leave the mural up for several days or place it in the hall as a depiction of class knowledge regarding a unit of study.

**WHO:**          Middle Grades

**WHEN:**         During a lesson

**THEME(S):**     People, Places, and Environments

- Over a period of time, have students research the climate, topography, and natural resources of a particular location. Have them draw a picture describing the characteristics of each location being researched.

**WHO:**          Middle Grades, High School

**WHEN:**         During a lesson

**THEME(S):**     People, Places, and Environment; Culture

- Have students visualize that they are immigrants coming to the North American colonies. Have them prepare a travel portfolio noting the physical characteristics of the northern, middle, and southern colonial regions. The portfolio should include an economic activity map, a physical features map, and a population density map that analyzes differences in development among the three regions. Using the maps and other research as evidence, have them select the region in which they would most like to live and write a position paper that describes their occupational choice and lifestyle during this era. Students' papers should be assessed based on how they illustrate their understanding of the patterns of settlement for each of the European powers that colonized North America.

**WHO:**  Middle Grades, High School

**WHEN:**  During a lesson

**THEME(S):**  Culture; Individual Development and Identity

- To help students understand the Egyptian culture and the important function of the afterlife, remind them that Egyptian royalty were buried with some of their most prized possessions. Have students pretend that upon their death, they are to be buried in a sarcophagus. Have them decide what prized personal possessions they would take with them into the afterlife such as stuffed animals or family photos. Then have them design their own sarcophagus out of construction paper or another medium of choice. Have them draw the personal items they wish to have placed into the sarcophagus and be prepared to tell the class what they decided to carry with them and why.

**WHO:**  Middle Grades, High School

**WHEN:**  During a lesson

**THEME(S):**  People, Places, and Environments; Individuals, Groups, and Institutions

- Have each student research one participant in the Underground Railroad. Students can choose a person who became well-known, such as Frederick Douglass, or someone lesser known, but just as important, such as William Still. Have students make posters presenting biographical information about their chosen figure and their contribution to the abolition movement. Students should feel free to get creative with their posters, adding pictures, maps, and writing samples. After completion of this task, students can set up their posters around the room to create an Underground Railroad *Gallery of Greats* for other students to view, even those from other classes. To get ideas and information for this activity, refer to the *Aboard the Underground Railroad* page on the National Park Service Web site at www.cr.nps.gov.

**WHO:**          Middle Grades, High School

**WHEN:**         During a lesson

**THEME(S):**     Time, Continuity, and Change

- Have students create an illustrated time line of events that represents a specific era in history.

**WHO:**          Middle Grades, High School

**WHEN:**         During a lesson

**THEME(S):**     People, Places, and Environments

- Have students create a relief map demonstrating their knowledge of physical geography by using salt dough (two parts salt, one part flour with enough water to make a very thick paste). Give students a list of features that must be included in their maps, such as lakes, bays, mountains, basins, mesas, and so forth. They can earn extra points for additional features such as fault lines and escarpments.

**WHO:**          Middle Grades, High School

**WHEN:**         After a lesson

**THEME(S):**     Individual Development and Identity; Individuals, Groups, and Institutions

- To assist students in recalling information regarding a person or group of people, have them draw a stick-person symbol. Have them attach notes about the person or group in eight areas to the appropriate spot on the figure; ideas to the brain, hopes or vision to the eyes, words to the mouth, actions to the hands, feelings to the heart, movement to the feet, weaknesses to the Achilles tendon, and strengths to the arm muscles (Sousa, 2006).

# REFLECTION AND APPLICATION

> How will I incorporate *drawing and artwork*
> into instruction to engage students' brains?

*Which drawing and artwork activities am I already incorporating
into my social studies curriculum?*

*What additional drawing and artwork activities will I incorporate?*

# Strategy 3

# Field Trips

## WHAT: DEFINING THE STRATEGY

My husband and I recently took a trip to the island of Jamaica to experience some much-needed rest and relaxation. Since we are always curious about the culture of the people wherever we visit, we spent one day of our vacation engaged in a field trip that turned out to be one of the most memorable parts of the trip. In the morning, we boarded a small bus and rode for $1\frac{1}{2}$ hours to several different destinations. During the ride, our tour guide, Rosalee, with a beautiful Jamaican accent, taught us some interesting facts about the culture of the country. Since Jamaica was once under British rule, it retains much of the British culture. In fact, many of the parishes have British names, such as London and Manchester. All schoolchildren wear colorful uniforms, but each school adopts a different one. In fact, you could tell which school a child attends by the uniform he or she is wearing. I found it interesting that parents pay a part of a child's tuition while the government pays the remaining part. Churches are plentiful in Jamaica and they are of all denominations—Roman Catholic, Seventh Day Adventist, Methodist, and so forth.

We arrived at our first destination, the Black River, where we boarded a boat and cruised down the water in search of crocodiles. We were not disappointed! Our boat tour guide was soon feeding pieces of chicken to crocodiles of all sizes, fondly named Philip, Barry, Tom, and Jerry. More important, I learned that crocodiles have been declared an endangered species and are protected by the government so they can no longer be hunted for their meat or their hides. By the way, the river was well-named since indeed it looked murky and black on the surface. But, when our boat guide took a cup and scooped water from the river, to our amazement, the water was crystal clear. We were told that it only looks black because the sediment on the bottom of the river is reflected in the water. We observed people making their living from the river, although the number-one industry in Jamaica is tourism. Some men were trapping shrimp using wicker baskets while others were retrieving crab traps that were brimming with their catch. We were told about the various trees and plants on the river and the purpose they serve for maintaining the equilibrium and stability of the river itself.

These were only tidbits of the many things my husband and I learned about Jamaica in that one day. By the way, on the river, we waved to a group of schoolchildren who happened to be taking the same field trip via another boat.

I call a field trip *a little bit of history wrapped in real packaging* since people remember what they see or experience in the real world far longer than they recall what they read about in class. Don't forget the option of virtual field trips that enable students to never leave the classroom and still visit places that would be inaccessible or cost-prohibitive.

## WHY: THEORETICAL FRAMEWORK

A valuable and time-honored part of the social studies curriculum is the field trip since it provides a real experience that makes the content more relevant (Melber & Hunter, 2010).

Electronic field trips can be more beneficial than real field trips because they expand the learning outside the walls of the classroom and students can experience an event more than one time (Gregory & Herndon, 2010).

The best learning occurs when students have an actual experience that taps into spatial memory and when they talk about the experience through dialogue and discussion (Fogarty, 2009).

Many museums actively engage learners in social studies content by using historical role plays or reenactments (Van Scotter, White, Hartoonian, & Davis, 2007).

To ensure a successful field-trip experience, teachers should know what is to be achieved by taking the field trip, focus the attention of students on those purposes during the field trip, and provide follow-up activities after the field trip (Chapin, 2005).

Actual and virtual field trips, during which students interact with sites outside their immediate environment, can help learners expand their purview (Melber & Hunter, 2010).

Taking students on a field trip is one way to integrate planned movement for learning into classroom content (Sprenger, 2007).

In the case of virtual field trips, teachers should model how to use the Web site prior to students using it and should have them work in pairs or groups to facilitate site navigation (Sunal & Haas, 2005).

Prior to starting a teaching unit, a field trip can be a very useful teaching tool, since students need the real-world, concrete examples that enable them to see, touch, and experience the world (Gregory & Parry, 2006).

Reducing the novelty effect of a field trip by preparing students ahead of time on what they will experience is a better way to support students' learning (Olson, Cox-Petersen, & McComas, 2001).

Thousands of years ago, two of the world's greatest teachers, Aristotle and Socrates, used field trips as tools of instruction (Krepel & Duvall, 1981).

# HOW: INSTRUCTIONAL ACTIVITIES

**WHO:**        Early and Middle Grades, High School

**WHEN:**       During a lesson

**THEME(S):**   All

- When the classroom does not provide enough space for movement or games, take the class outside the four walls of the room and engage them in purposeful movement to reinforce a social studies concept or play a game. For example, you could engage students in a game of capture the flag to simulate the Civil War. Not only will this *field trip* provide more space in which to engage students; it will also supply their brains with Vitamin D from the sun, which is needed for healthy brain and body development and which many of today's students sorely lack. Even when not playing a game, taking students outside and convening class under a tree on a beautiful day can provide much needed novelty for their brains.

**WHO:**        Early and Middle Grades, High School

**WHEN:**       Before and after a lesson

**THEME(S):**   All

- Prior to taking a real or virtual field trip, work with students to complete the K-N-L (know, need to know, learned) graphic organizer in Chapter 5 to find out what students already know about the place to be visited. Write their responses on the board. Then have students brainstorm what they think they will want or need to know or discover during the field trip. This is written in column two. Take the field trip. Finally, after the culmination of the field trip, complete the last column by having students discuss what they learned during the field trip.

**WHO:**　　　　Middle Grades, High School

**WHEN:**　　　Before and during a lesson

**THEME(S):**　All

- Have students emulate the work of an ethnographer by observing and describing one area of their school, including the entrance to the building, the front office, the principal's office, the cafeteria, the halls when students are changing classes, and the media center. Have students, like the social scientist, gather data, select and interpret the relevant data, and reflect on the findings as well as the process of collection. Then have them write a description of what they have observed for a specific audience, such as students who will attend the school in 2020, a visitor from another country, or any other target audience they select (Melber & Hunter, 2010).

**WHO:**　　　　Early Grades

**WHEN:**　　　Before a lesson

**THEME(S):**　People, Places, and Environments

- So that students have an opportunity to experience what it is like to live in their community, take them on a walking field trip of the neighborhood around the school. Have them notice main and cross street signs. Have them look for apartments, condominiums, or homes as well as restaurants, gas stations, places of worship, grocery stores, and government provided services, such as fire stations. When you return to the classroom, have students tell or describe in writing what they have seen. This should lead to a discussion of the physical and human characteristics of the community; increase the geography, civics, and economic connections in students' brains; and determine what businesses are not currently a part of the community that they might like to open as future entrepreneurs.

**WHO:**　　　　Early and Middle Grades, High School

**WHEN:**　　　Before a lesson

**THEME(S):**　All

- Plan and take students on a field trip to a history or other type of museum to view exhibits and artifacts related to a social studies unit of study. Contrary to popular belief, this field trip should probably be taken prior to the unit of study so that students can make real-world connections to the content as the unit is taught.

**WHO:**　　　　Early and Middle Grades, High School

**WHEN:**　　　Before a lesson

**THEME(S):**　All

- To add some fun and provide purpose, prior to taking your students on a field trip, visit the location in advance and plan a scavenger hunt so that when students arrive they can search for predetermined artifacts or find the answers to prearranged questions during the field trip itself. Give small prizes to students who are able to locate everything listed on the scavenger hunt. Be certain that scavenger hunts remain focused on standards-based content.

**WHO:**        Early and Middle Grades, High School

**WHEN:**        Before a lesson

**THEME(S):**        Culture; People, Places, and Environments

- Put students in cooperative groups of four to six. Assign each group a different state, country, or continent, depending on whether the objective of the lesson is local, national, or international. Have each group plan a *field trip* that will *carry* the remaining members of the class to that location. Groups can be creative about how they will present the information, but they must provide firsthand experiences for students regarding the culture of the location. In other words, groups cannot simply write and orally read a report to the class about the location. That is boring! When groups finish the presentation, students must feel that they have actually been transported to that place!

**WHO:**        Early and Middle Grades, High School

**WHEN:**        Before a lesson

**THEME(S):**        All

- When students cannot feasibly visit a given place or time, have the time come to them. Invite guest speakers to class who can talk about their personal experiences of having lived through a specific period of history or a different time or culture. Parents of students of diversity make wonderful resources. There are also presenters whose job it is to fully assume the persona of a famous historical figure and who can come to your class and tell their personal story while fully attired in authentic dress of the time period. These people can make a lasting impression on the memories of your students, particularly if their stories are funny or emotional!

**WHO:**        Early and Middle Grades, High School

**WHEN:**        Before, during, and after a lesson

**THEME(S):**        All

- Providing students with a focus prior to taking a field trip is essential. This focus can be facilitated by generating questions that students will be using to guide the field trip experience. These questions should not be just knowledge or comprehension questions but should include some at the analysis, synthesis, and evaluation levels. Refer to Chapter 1: Brainstorming and Discussion to find question stems from Bloom's Taxonomy that can be used to formulate these questions. Following the field trip, the answers to the questions should be discussed.

**WHO:**       Early and Middle Grades, High School

**WHEN:**      During a class

**THEME(S):**  All

- Have students experience what it is like to visit locations of interest around the globe and never leave the classroom via a virtual field trip. Go online to Web sites and access virtual field trips that pertain to a social studies concept being taught. Allow students to work in pairs or small groups. Model for students how to use the Web site or provide written directions. An example of one such site is http://icom.museum, a virtual library of museums from around the world.

# REFLECTION AND APPLICATION

How will I incorporate *field trips* into instruction to engage students' brains?

*Which field trips am I already incorporating into my social studies curriculum?*

*What additional field trips will I incorporate?*

# Strategy 4

# Games

## WHAT: DEFINING THE STRATEGY

It is several days prior to the social studies test on Friday. Since Mrs. Stewart has been using brain-compatible strategies to teach the content throughout the unit, students are confident that they will do well. However, the brain needs repetition; therefore, a spirited game would be a great vehicle for review prior to testing. Today, as students file into the classroom, the music from the game show *Jeopardy* is playing. Mrs. Stewart has created the game to review the most important concepts in the chapter.

The class is divided into three heterogeneous teams. Each team selects a captain who provides the responses to the emcee after the team has put their heads together to come up with the appropriate question, and a scribe who keeps track of the points and writes down the wager and the answer for the bonus round. Mrs. Stewart has selected key ideas from a chapter and turned them into answers for the *Jeopardy* board. Three answers are placed into five columns with the easiest answers worth $100 each and the most difficult, $500. Teams then compete against one another by selecting an answer from a specific row and increment of money and providing the accompanying question. If the question is correct, the designated amount of money is added to the score. If the question is incorrect, the amount is subtracted from the score. To make the game more interesting, two answers have been designated as *daily doubles.* Play continues according to the rules of the television game show until all the answers have been selected or until time runs out. All teams can wager any or all of their monies on a bonus answer, which should be the most difficult answer from the chapter. The team with the most money at the end of the game wins, or, to be less competitive, any team that acquires more money than a predetermined amount, such as $2,000, wins (Tate, 2010).

This game can also be played via the computer, but whatever format is used, it is one example of how the strategy of games can be used to engage students' brains in a fun and motivating way. For additional examples, read on!

---

## WHY: THEORETICAL FRAMEWORK

The competition of a game can increase students' speed in recall tasks and makes learning fun but is most effective when students are at similar ability levels (Algozzine, Campbell, & Wang, 2009a).

A game can inject fun and laughter into the lesson and helps students take risks in front of their peers (Udvari-Solner & Kluth, 2008).

Since games, puzzles, and other fun activities can make the content more creative, they should be used when students have to memorize, practice, or rehearse crucial information (Caine, Caine, McClintic, & Klimek, 2009).

The amount of time students are exposed to and involved with content is doubled when they develop the content of the game first and then play it (Allen, 2008a).

Pairing cooperative learning with games helps students focus and pay attention, encourages them to cooperate with one another, and is effective, motivating, and fun (Algozzine, Campbell, & Wang, 2009b).

If games are going to represent a way to review, then they must focus on the academic content (Marzano, 2007).

Many of the games we learned as kids can be adapted by teachers and used in the classroom to bring content to life while having students physically moving (Baumgarten, 2006).

If conducted with care and structured properly, physically engaging games can greatly increase learning for students of all ages (Allen, 2008a).

Physical games engage both children and adults at many different levels: mentally, emotionally, and socially (Summerford, 2000).

In an analysis of 93 studies, the use of games during instruction was found to increase student achievement by 14 percentile points (Walberg, 1999).

---

## HOW: INSTRUCTIONAL ACTIVITIES

**WHO:**          Early and Middle Grades, High School

**WHEN:**         Before or during a lesson

**THEME(S):**     Culture

- Have students work in cooperative groups of four to six to research various cultures for determining what games the children or teenagers of those cultures play. Have them select one game from one culture and learn the rules for playing it. Then have them take turns involving the entire class in playing the game. When debriefing following the playing of the cultural game, have students discuss possible indicators the game provides regarding important values held by the culture.

**WHO:**　　　Early and Middle Grades, High School

**WHEN:**　　During a lesson

**THEME(S):**　All

- During a class discussion or a review activity, ask a question of the entire class. Give the class time to think of the answer. Then toss a *Nerf* or any other soft ball to one student who is to respond to the question. If the student's answer is correct, he or she can select the student who is to answer the next question and toss the ball to that student. If the student's answer is incorrect, he or she must toss the ball back to you so that you can select the next student to respond. A plastic Frisbee also works well. Be sure to ask the question of the entire class before you or another student selects someone to catch the ball and answer the next question. Then allow the selected student time to think of the answer (a minimum of 5 seconds).

**WHO:**　　　Early and Middle Grades, High School

**WHEN:**　　During a lesson

**THEME(S):**　All

- Have students work in cooperative groups to construct an original game board according to the following guidelines: The game must provide at least 30 spaces, including *begin* and *end* spaces, two *move ahead* spaces, and two *go back* spaces. Have students make game question cards appropriate to whatever content needs to be reviewed with an accompanying answer key. Have groups switch game boards and answer keys. Each group reviews content by rolling a number generator (die) or number wheel, moving the number of spaces designated, selecting a card, and answering the designated question on the card. If the answer is correct, the student moves the number of spaces indicated. If the answer is incorrect, the student stays put. The first student in each group to get to the end of the game board wins (Tate, 2010).

**WHO:**　　　Early and Middle Grades, High School

**WHEN:**　　During a lesson

**THEME(S):**　All

- Write social studies vocabulary words or concepts that are capable of being acted out on index cards. Engage students in a spirited game of *charades* by having them take turns coming to the front of the room and, without looking, selecting a word card, and acting out the definition of the word. The student cannot speak or write but must gesture to role play the word. The first student in the class to guess the word gets a point. The student who accumulates the most points by the end of the game wins, and, as a side benefit, the class gets a review of social studies content.

**WHO:**          Early and Middle Grades, High School

**WHEN:**         During a lesson

**THEME(S):**     All

- Write social studies vocabulary words or concepts that are capable of being drawn on index cards. Have students play the game of *Pictionary* by having them take turns coming to the front of the room and, without looking, selecting a word card and drawing a picture that depicts the meaning of the concept on the dry-erase board, document camera, and so forth. The first student in the class to guess the word gets a point and can elect to draw the next word. The student who has the most points in an allotted time wins the game.

**WHO:**          Early and Middle Grades, High School

**WHEN:**         During a lesson

**THEME(S):**     All

- Engage students in a spirited game of *BINGO* as a review activity by having them draw a 3 × 3 matrix on a piece of paper. Have them make the nine boxes large enough to write a social studies vocabulary word in each box. Provide students with a list of 12 to 15 words that you have previously taught. Have students write any nine of the words in the boxes on their papers. Then write the definitions of the words on index cards and place them in a plastic bag or box. Have students take turns reaching into the bag, pulling out a definition, and reading it loud enough for the entire class to hear. As the definition is read, students mark the matching word on their card with an X. The first student who marks all four words in the corners of a card shouts the word *BINGO!* However, before the student is declared the winner, he or she must name each word to be sure it was called and then give the definition of each word in his or her own words. If the student is incapable of doing this, then the game continues until another student shouts *BINGO!* If you want the same cards to be used repeatedly, then students should cover the words with chips made out of construction paper or anything else that would suffice.

**WHO:**          Early and Middle Grades, High School

**WHEN:**         During a lesson

**THEME(S):**     All

- Divide the class into two heterogeneous groups. Have two students from each group come to the front of the room and become partners. Give one person in each pair the same social studies vocabulary word. Their job is to get their partner to guess the word by giving them a one-word clue. Gestures and proper nouns are not allowed. One pair begins. The point value begins at 10 and decreases by one each time the word is not guessed. If the first pair does not guess the word, play proceeds to the other pair for nine points. Play continues until the word is guessed or until it has been played down to five points. The point value at the time the word is guessed goes to the group that the pair represents and four other students come to the front of the room to play the next word. The first group to reach a predetermined number of points is the winner. This game is played like the television show *Password*.

| | |
|---|---|
| **WHO:** | Early and Middle Grades, High School |
| **WHEN:** | During a lesson |
| **THEME(S):** | All |

- Have students play the game *Who Am I?* by providing written clues regarding a famous historical figure already taught. Have students take turns reading their clues aloud as their peers attempt to guess the identity of the figure. The first student to guess the figure wins the point. If no student is able to identify the figure, then the student providing the clues gets the point.

| | |
|---|---|
| **WHO:** | Early and Middle Grades, High School |
| **WHEN:** | During a lesson |
| **THEME(S):** | All |

- Purchase the CD *Classic TV Game Show Themes* so that you have the music that will accompany many of the games that you will be playing with your students. This CD contains the themes from game shows such as *Jeopardy!, Wheel of Fortune, The Price Is Right, Password, Family Feud,* and many more.

| | |
|---|---|
| **WHO:** | Early and Middle Grades |
| **WHEN:** | During a lesson |
| **THEME(S):** | All |

- Consult the series *Engage the Brain Games* for additional game ideas in the area of social studies. Books for Grades K through 5 are cross-curricular, including games in the area of social studies. There is a separate social studies book for Grades 6 through 8. Consult the Corwin Web site at www.corwin.com for information.

# REFLECTION AND APPLICATION

How will I incorporate *games* into
instruction to engage students' brains?

**Which games am I already incorporating into my social studies curriculum?**

**What additional games will I incorporate?**

# Graphic Organizers, Semantic Maps, and Word Webs

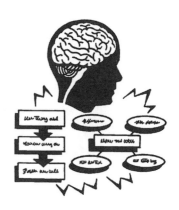

## WHAT: DEFINING THE STRATEGY

In the Introduction of the best seller *Worksheets Don't Grow Dendrites* (2nd ed.), I tell the true story of teaching a lesson to a group of middle school students on the three branches of the federal government. One of the first activities in the lesson was to teach students about the three branches using a graphic organizer. As I discussed the function of each branch and which positions were in it, I drew a mind map (shown at the top of page 44) on the board. Students were required to draw the same map in their notes.

This graphic organizer and the movement activity that followed ensured that every student knew the branches of the government, what each branch did, and which positions were in the branch by the time I completed my lesson. By the way, the second part of this lesson is described in the Instructional Activity section of Chapter 10: Movement. If this is a concept you must teach, please teach it this way. I promise you, it works!

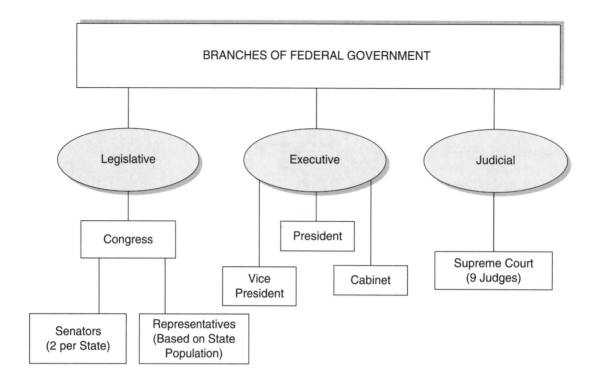

## WHY: THEORETICAL FRAMEWORK

Graphic organizers increase the thinking skills of students since they enable them to make connections to information and break that information into chunks that are manageable (Gregory & Herndon, 2010).

To assist struggling students, particularly English language learners, graphic organizers or fill-in-the-blank guides should be given prior to a lecture and filled in by students during the lecture (Sousa, 2011).

Thinking maps have the following five critical attributes: (1) a consistent form that reflects the skill being addressed; (2) a flexible way the map can be configured; (3) a developmental form that can increase in complexity; (4) an integration of content knowledge with thinking processes; and (5) a reflection of the learner's thinking processes (Hyerle & Alper, 2011).

For students who are strong in the visual modality or those who think graphically rather than linearly, graphic organizers are excellent teaching tools (Perez, 2008).

*Graphic organizers make thinking and learning visible* (Fogarty, 2009, p. 112).

Graphic organizers, pictures, graphs, and charts are effective tools by which students can organize patterns since images are more easily remembered by the brain than are words (Feinstein, 2009).

Graphic organizers can be used not only as prereading and prewriting tools; since they facilitate discussion and note taking, they can be used following the reading of narrative and expository texts as summary or synthesis tools (Perez, 2008).

Curriculum graphic organizers assist adolescents in doing the following: establishing prior knowledge, delineating the main concepts and deleting the unimportant, classifying and organizing facts, assisting students with note taking, and summarizing and increasing their thinking skills (Karten, 2009).

When students create their own graphic organizers, they create visuals that make the content more memorable since they conceptualize and design the organizer and, therefore, know the content intimately (Allen, 2008a).

Graphic organizers enhance both comprehension and memory and, therefore, serve as powerful learning tools for all students (DiCecco & Gleason, 2002).

Graphic organizers enable students to think as they read, which increases memory and assists them in comprehending a story in parts and as a whole (Algozzine, Campbell, & Wang, 2009a).

# HOW: INSTRUCTIONAL ACTIVITIES

**WHO:**  Early Grades

**WHEN:**  During a lesson

**THEME(S):**  People, Places, and Environments

- Have students examine recent and past population data for the following categories of people: their own classroom, elementary school, local community, city, state, and country. Have them design a table that compares the data and discuss why the changes may have occurred (National Council for the Social Studies, 2010).

**WHO:**  Early and Middle Grades, High School

**WHEN:**  Before and after a lesson

**THEME(S):**  All

- Create a picture graphic organizer, or if your students are old enough, have them create one. For example, students could draw a ship on which to take notes regarding explorers they are learning about, or they could draw a road with stop signs to denote the road to a revolution. On this road, students could record causes leading to the Revolutionary War.

**WHO:**        Early and Middle Grades, High School

**WHEN:**       Before and after a lesson

**THEME(S):**   All

- To access students' prior knowledge and summarize content following a lesson, have students complete a K-N-L (know, need to know, learned) chart. Have students discuss or brainstorm (1) what they already *know* about a concept or unit of study; (2) what they will *need* to know to really understand the concept; and (3) following instruction, what they have *learned*.

| The K-N-L Strategy | | |
|---|---|---|
| Topic: | | |
| What I Know | What I Need to Know | What I Learned |
| | | |
| | | |
| | | |
| | | |
| | | |
| | | |

**WHO:**        Early and Middle Grades, High School

**WHEN:**       During a lesson

**THEME(S):**   All

- Have students clarify the meanings of concepts and identify connections to other related words by using the sample semantic word map below. Determine a central social studies concept to be taught, and place it in the circle. Have students brainstorm a list of words to connect with the concept, such as bigger ideas, events, attributes of the word, or examples and have them explain how these new words relate to the concept and place them on the map. Ask students to share and explain their maps in a small group, justifying the reasons for their choice of words.

## Semantic Word Map

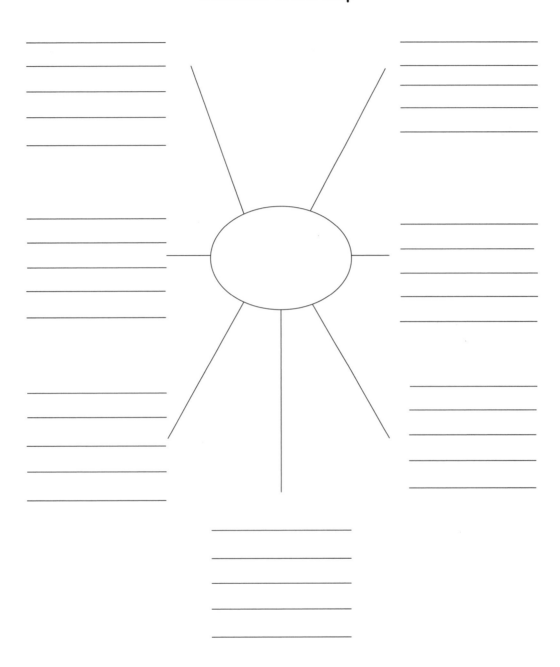

**WHO:**        Middle Grades, High School

**WHEN:**       During a lesson

**THEME(S):**   People, Places, and Environments

- There are probably more cause-effect relationships in social studies than in any other concept area, with the possible exception of science. Have students identify these relationships by completing the Cause/Effect graphic organizer on page 48.

## Cause/Effect

So

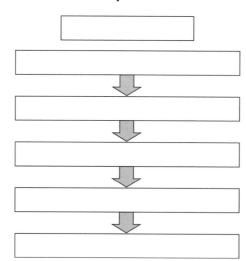

**WHO:**        Early and Middle Grades, High School

**WHEN:**       During a lesson

**THEME(S):**   All

- Whenever students have to place historical events in sequential order, have them use the Sequence graphic organizer below.

## Sequence

**WHO:**        Elementary and Middle Grades, High School

**WHEN:**       During a lesson

**THEME(S):**   Power, Authority, and Governance; Global Connections

- Have students use the Venn diagram below to compare and contrast various social studies concepts such as (1) the different forms of governance by examining the similarities and differences in their constitutions or (2) the language, art, music, and belief systems in two diverse cultures, or (3) the Declaration of Independence and the philosophy of John Locke.

## Compare/Contrast

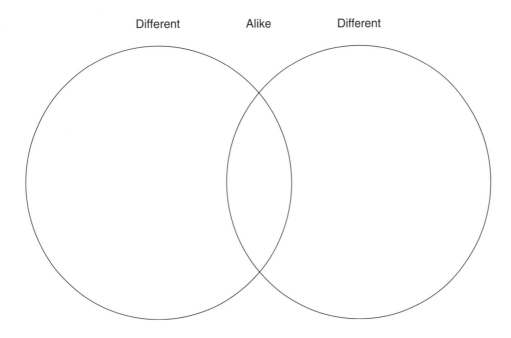

Different          Alike          Different

**WHO:**        Middle Grades, High School

**WHEN:**       During a lesson

**THEME(S):**   Production, Distribution, and Consumption

- Have students peruse the newspaper or the Internet to find news stories about taxes. Using the following graphic organizer, have them create a 5*W*'s **and an *H*** summary for at least one of the stories. This summary should answer the questions *who, what, when, where, why,* and *how.* For instance, summaries could answer the following:

  o Who pays the tax?
  o Who collects the tax?
  o What are the taxes for?
  o When are they due?
  o Where are they collected or assessed?
  o Why are they needed?
  o On average, how much do people pay?
  o How do people feel about the tax?

  This graphic organizer can be used for any number of purposes such as reading a textbook chapter or listening to a news report on television.

## 5W's and an H

*Use the organizer below to create a "5Ws and an H" summary.*

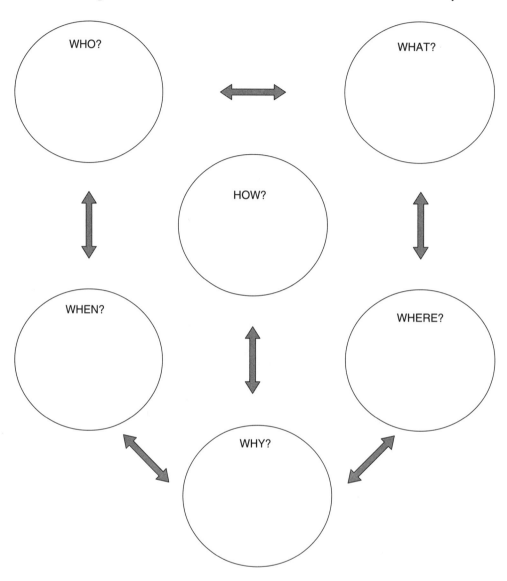

**WHO:**          Early and Middle Grades, High School

**WHEN:**         During a lesson

**THEME(S):**     All

- While lecturing or discussing social studies ideas with students, complete a semantic, concept, or mind map on the board as a visual of how the major concepts are related to one another. Have students copy the map in their notes as you explain each part. See the sample format below:

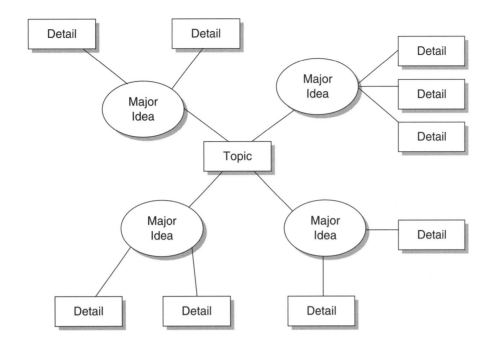

**WHO:**         Middle Grades, High School

**WHEN:**        During a lesson

**THEME(S):**    Power, Authority, and Governance

- Have students create a *What's What* directory of politics. Have them read current news items related to a political issues and identify at least five important issues. Have them use the chart below to list these issues as the main headings across the top. Then have them identify several politicians or civic leaders whose views differ on the issues selected. Have them list the leaders' names along the side and summarize the leaders' views under each issue heading.

## What's What: A Political Directory

| Politicians' Names | Main Issues | | | | |
|---|---|---|---|---|---|
| | | | | | |
| | | | | | |
| | | | | | |
| | | | | | |

**WHO:**        Middle Grades, High School

**WHEN:**        During a lesson

**THEME(S):**        Power, Authority, and Governance

- Explain to students that historically each level of government has performed certain services and that there are differences in the kinds of service responsibilities at the local, state, and national levels. Have students research the newspaper, Internet, and so forth and identify as many services as possible that are performed by individuals representing the three levels of government. Then have them complete the chart below listing the services provided.

## "Service, Please"

| Level | Services |
|---|---|
| LOCAL | |
| STATE | |
| NATIONAL | |

**WHO:**        Middle Grades, High School

**WHEN:**        During a lesson

**THEME(S):**        Power, Authority, and Governance

- After reading major news stories for at least a week, have students list the major problems faced by individuals in local, state, and national government. Complete the chart below showing how various problems relate to governmental officials at all three levels. Have students repeat this activity later in the school year to ascertain whether the problems or issues have changed.

## Major Governmental Issues

| Major Problems Faced | | | | |
|---|---|---|---|---|
| LOCAL | | | | |
| STATE | | | | |
| NATIONAL | | | | |

**WHO:**      Middle Grades, High School

**WHEN:**     During a lesson

**THEME(S):**    Production, Distribution, and Consumption

- Explain to students that competition typically involves a contest between two or more individuals or groups in order to win some prize or gain some advantage. However, in an American free-enterprise economic system, competition involves the rivalry between two or more business enterprises to sell some particular goods or services. Have students examine the advertisements in the newspaper or on the Internet and identify at least five types of businesses where there is a good deal of competition. In addition, have them identify five businesses that appear to have little competition. Have them use the chart below to list the businesses they have identified.

# To Compete or Not to Compete

Examine the advertisements in a newspaper. Identify at least five types of businesses where there is a good deal of competition and five businesses that appear to have very little competition.

| A Good Deal of Competition | Very Little Competition |
|---|---|
|  |  |
|  |  |
|  |  |
|  |  |
|  |  |

**WHO:**        Middle Grades, High School

**WHEN:**       During a lesson

**THEME(S):**   Production, Distribution, and Consumption

- Involve students in a discussion of the four types of economic systems (traditional, command, market, and mixed). Have them locate current articles in the newspaper or on the Internet that show examples of each type. Have them complete the chart below with the appropriate information.

## Economic Systems

Complete the chart below by filling in the appropriate information underneath each economic system.

| | Traditional | Command | Market | Mixed |
|---|---|---|---|---|
| Ownership of Property | | | | |
| Distribution of Income | | | | |
| Role of Government | | | | |
| Role of Economic Incentives | | | | |

**WHO:**　　　　Middle Grades

**WHEN:**　　　During a lesson

**THEME(S):**　　People, Places, and Environments

- Over a period of time, have students research the climate, topography, and natural resources of a particular location. Have them make a chart similar to the one below describing the characteristics of each location.

| Location | Climate | Topography | Natural Resources |
|---|---|---|---|
|  |  |  |  |
|  |  |  |  |
|  |  |  |  |

**WHO:**        Middle Grades

**WHEN:**       During a lesson

**THEME(S):**   Individuals, Groups, and Institutions

- Have students conduct research on the most practiced religions in the world. Have them fill in a graphic organizer similar to the one in the activity above, but rather than *Location*, this organizer would reflect *Religions of the World*. The other categories could include *Founders, Holy Days, Holy Books, Houses of Worship*, and *Primary Locations.*

**WHO:**        Middle Grades, High School

**WHEN:**       During a lesson

**THEME(S):**   People, Places, and Environments

- Have students develop tables where they compare the population data from several nations. Have them discuss the effects of the data on the environment and societal issues in that nation.

**WHO:**        Early and Middle Grades

**WHEN:**       During a lesson

**THEME(S):**   All

- Refer to the series *Engage the Brain: Graphic Organizers and Other Visual Strategies* for additional graphic organizer ideas in the area of social studies. Books for Grades K through 5 are cross-curricular, including graphic organizers and visuals in the area of social studies. There is a separate social studies book for Grades 6 through 8. Consult the Corwin Web site at www.corwin.com for information.

# REFLECTION AND APPLICATION

How will I incorporate *graphic organizers, semantic maps, and word webs* into instruction to engage students' brains?

*Which graphic organizers, semantic maps, and word webs am I already incorporating into my social studies curriculum?*

*What additional activities will I incorporate?*

# Strategy 6

# Humor

## WHAT: DEFINING THE STRATEGY

*If April showers bring May flowers,
what do May flowers bring?* Pilgrims

*What flower does not grow in
the ground?* The Mayflower

*What did Tennessee (Tenness see)?* The
same thing that Arkansas (Arkan saw).

*What did Delaware (Della wear)?* She wore
her brand New Jersey (new jersey).

Most brains of younger children do not get jokes. The frontal lobe is not developed enough to comprehend the subtleties in the language of humor. However, by the time students get to middle and high school, most classrooms have a *class clown*. The job of the class clown is to bring in jokes and riddles that could be told periodically either before, during, or after instruction. If the riddles or jokes are related to the subject area being taught, similar to the ones listed above, their value is increased. However, even if they are generic, humor is still very valuable to a brain-compatible classroom. Laughter puts the brain in a positive state and increases the likelihood that the content being taught will be remembered. After all, remember the saying *The brain learns best when it is not in high stress*! Low to moderate stress is actually good for learning, but high stress is a threat to the brain and it shuts the brain down to higher-level thinking. It is also the reason that people have to be treated for posttraumatic stress disorder.

In all of my books, I warn against confusing humor with sarcasm. There are teachers who make comments that demean or belittle students and believe that this practice is funny. Even though other students may laugh, sarcasm is never funny! Even if the student that the sarcastic remark is directed to laughs, the laughter may be designed to hide the hurt feelings that the student is actually experiencing. After all, students have to save face in front of one another. Just remember that the literal definition of the word sarcasm is *a tearing of the flesh.* Although there is research to support that laughter can heal, there is just as much research to support that high stress can kill, both physically and psychologically.

## WHY: THEORETICAL FRAMEWORK

The emotional climate in the classroom has so much to do with how much students can learn and humor and music are key ingredients in enhancing students' emotional states (Lengel & Kuczala, 2010).

*Humor is creativity plus play* and enables students to link learning with positive feelings, which can result in an increased love of learning (Jensen & Nickelsen, 2008, p. 53).

Humor is one way that teachers can provide novelty in the classroom since students will often talk about the humorous experience, thereby reviewing the content learned while laughing (Allen, 2008a).

Humor and laughter in the classroom can result in healthier teachers, decreased anxiety in students, improved receptivity to difficult material, enhanced recall, and creative thinking, as well as improved student-teacher relationships (Jensen & Nickelsen, 2008).

People who have a humorous frame of mind thrive on recognizing incongruity and absurdities, satire, and irony and are able to laugh at themselves as well (Costa, 2008).

A person's imagination should be given permission to create in ways that are humorous, fun, surreal, and absurd (Markowitz & Jensen, 2007).

When teachers periodically use humor, they provide a sense of cooperation and show concern for students (Gettinger & Kohler, 2006).

Humor frees up creativity and fosters the higher level thinking skills of anticipation, visual imagery, creating analogies, and the ability to recognize novel relationships from various vantage points (Costa, 2008).

Students are likely to adopt the same general attitude in class as their teacher when the teacher projects an enthusiastic and positive demeanor (Gettinger & Kohler, 2006).

The sense of humor of older adolescents becomes more sophisticated and teachers can become the brunt of this ability (Santrock, 2003).

# HOW: INSTRUCTIONAL ACTIVITIES

**WHO:**        Middle Grades, High School

**WHEN:**       During a lesson

**THEME(S):**   All

- Laugh at yourself! A teacher who is able to make fun of herself seems to be a teacher that most students love. This act alone helps you appear human and more approachable and will go a long way toward helping you develop a relationship with your students. However, although you will also want to laugh with your students, you should never laugh at them!

**WHO:**        Middle Grades, High School

**WHEN:**       During a lesson

**THEME(S):**   All

- Select appropriate cartoons, jokes, or riddles and integrate them into your social studies lessons. You may even want to begin each social studies lesson with a joke or riddle. One geography teacher related the following story to me regarding his use of humor. He was teaching the concept of plate tectonics, or the shifting of the earth's plates. He taught his class that there is a place in Africa where the plates collide. It is called Djibouti. When he finished teaching them about the cracks in Djibouti, no student in his class would ever forget that lesson. If you don't get this joke, have someone explain it to you!

**WHO:**        Middle Grades, High School

**WHEN:**       Before or after a lesson

**THEME(S):**   All

- Appoint a *class clown*. The job of the class clown is to bring in a week's worth of jokes or riddles to be shared with the class. I personally like riddles better than jokes, since brains often have to think at very high levels to understand riddles. Be certain that you read over and give your approval to each joke or riddle so that no inappropriate ones are shared. Stop periodically and have the *class clown* share with the class. Then get back to work on the class content. The laughter will put all brains in a more positive state and will accelerate the learning. The role of the class clown can change at the end of a week and another student can assume this responsibility.

**WHO:**        Early and Middle Grades, High School

**WHEN:**       Before or after a lesson

**THEME(S):**   All

- Have all students bring in riddles and jokes and place them in a class box. During an appropriate time, have one student go to the box, select a riddle or joke, and read it to the entire class. Remember to read all of the entries ahead of time so that no inappropriate selections end up in the box. In the case of more challenging riddles, you may want to give students time to come up with the answer, even allowing them to bring the answer in the next day so that they can share the riddle with the family at home. Points could be awarded to anyone who comes up with the correct answer.

**WHO:**        Early and Middle Grades, High School

**WHEN:**       During a lesson

**THEME(S):**   All

- When selecting students to fulfill roles during a social studies cooperative learning activity, use humorous categories like the following:

  o Students wearing blue (or any other color)
  o Students wearing the most jewelry
  o Students who have the most siblings
  o Students who live closest or farthest from school
  o Students wearing glasses or contact lenses (Tate, 2010)

**WHO:**        Early and Middle Grades, High School

**WHEN:**       During a lesson

**THEME(S):**   All

- Have students celebrate and support the appropriate answers of other classmates in the following ways:

  o Applause
  o Thumbs-up
  o High fives
  o Standing ovations
  o Original cheers

  Consult Chapter 17: Celebrations in the book *Shouting Won't Grow Dendrites: 20 Techniques for Managing a Brain-Compatible Classroom* for at least 25 additional ways to celebrate the success of students in the social studies classroom (Tate, 2007).

**WHO:**        Early and Middle Grades, High School

**WHEN:**       Before, during, and after a lesson

**THEME(S):**   All

- Since messages cross the synapse faster when the brain is thinking positively, place humorous or positive signs around the classroom so that when students are not looking at you, they are experiencing some encouraging peripherals. Signs could include the following: *If you believe you can, or you believe you can't, you are right!* or *Success comes in cans, not in can'ts.*

| | |
|---|---|
| **WHO:** | Middle Grades, High School |
| **WHEN:** | During a lesson |
| **THEME(S):** | All |

- Most editorial or political cartoons from newspapers and magazines deal with timely social and political issues. Collect relevant editorial or political cartoons to integrate into your lessons or have your students collect them and bring them to class. Put a cartoon under the document camera so that all the class can see it and give them time to think individually or with a partner to interpret the idea that the cartoon is attempting to get across. Be sure to find clues that will help in deciphering the cartoons, such as looking for symbols in them. The Web site www.cagle.com offers a great collection of political cartoons arranged by artists' names and states.

| | |
|---|---|
| **WHO:** | Middle Grades, High School |
| **WHEN:** | After a lesson |
| **THEME(S):** | All |

- Have students create their own comic book character or superhero based on an important historical figure. The comic book should reflect the contributions of the superhero to society or delineate the way in which he or she has changed the world.

| | |
|---|---|
| **WHO:** | Middle Grades, High School |
| **WHEN:** | After a lesson |
| **THEME(S):** | All |

- If you want to give students' brains a challenge, have them create their own riddles or jokes based on social studies content that has been taught. This can be given as a homework assignment or extra credit provided for any student who creates an original riddle or joke and shares it with the class. You would be surprised at how truly creative some of your students are.

# REFLECTION AND APPLICATION

How will I incorporate *humor* into
instruction to engage students' brains?

**Which humorous activities am I already incorporating into my social studies curriculum?**

**What additional activities will I incorporate?**

# Strategy 7

# Manipulatives, Experiments, Labs, and Models

## WHAT: DEFINING THE STRATEGY

There is an activity called *concept attainment* that not only uses cards as manipulatives but also fosters higher level thinking skills. To implement concept attainment, think of a social studies concept that you wish to teach. Write the words *YES* and *NO* on separate cards and place them in separate columns on the board. Think of terms that are attributes of the concept and terms that are not, write the terms on separate index cards, and pass them out randomly to students in class. Do not tell students what the original concept is. The object is for students to guess the concept by considering positive and negative examples of it. The teacher needs to provide the first few examples by placing two or three words under the *YES* or *NO* columns.

For example, let's say that the original concept is *democracy*. The first term on the card is the word *equality*. That would be placed under the *YES*, since it is a positive example of *democracy*. The word *protection* would also be a *YES*. The word *dictator* would be a *NO*. Before any student is allowed to guess the concept, have students take turns coming to the front of the room, showing their word to the class, and having students predict whether it would be a *YES* or a *NO*. Have the student place the word in the appropriate column. If the class answers incorrectly, correct them. When you feel that most students know the concept, have them write it down on a piece of paper. Students love when the concept is finally revealed! You can also add a little drama by slowly revealing the answer. When that concept is guessed, select another concept and begin with a new group of terms given to students who did not participate with the last concept. Just having students hold and manipulate the cards on the board adds another dimension to this activity and takes advantage of the natural connection between the hands and the brain.

# WHY: THEORETICAL FRAMEWORK

Artifacts, or objects made by human beings, can be found at garage sales of family members or swap meets, and can prove unique or novel to students (Melber & Hunter, 2010).

Whatever the age or grade level, content area, and ability or disability, many students need to see, touch, and manipulate the conceptual underpinnings of the concepts being taught (Algozzine, Campbell, & Wang, 2009b).

Using a wide variety of manipulatives provides kinesthetic-tactile opportunities for adolescents to *touch and be touched by the concepts* they are learning in a lesson (Karten, 2009).

Teachers should provide chances for students to *hold, mold, and manipulate clay or other objects* since activity and exercise can facilitate the growth of new cells in the brain (Jensen, 2008, p. 38).

Students increase their abilities to verbalize their thinking, discuss ideas, take ownership, and find answers to problems on their own when they use manipulatives over time (Sebesta & Martin, 2004).

The best way for even young students to learn the definition of a map is to have them create their own simple maps (Sunal & Haas, 2005).

Making physical models is one activity that aids students in the nonlinguistic (or mental) processing of information (Marzano, 2007).

It is necessary for students to understand the following five skills if they are to comprehend maps and mapping: (1) directional orientation, (2) map scales, (3) place location, (4) location expression, and (5) map symbols (Parker, 2009).

In many middle and high school classrooms, teachers do not use manipulatives, yet that is the time they are needed most in order to make those abstract concepts concrete for adolescents who do not have the prior knowledge to understand them (Karten, 2009).

The relationship between the hands and brain activity is so complicated that no single theory adequately explains it (Jensen, 2001).

# HOW: INSTRUCTIONAL ACTIVITIES

**WHO:**     Early and Middle Grades, High School

**WHEN:**    During a lesson

**THEME(S):**    All

- Have students hold up response cards when answering social studies questions in class. These can be in the form of a dry erase board, which can be erased with a sock that students bring from home, or, in the absence of this type of board, discarded copy paper can be used. Students write down their short answers to selected social studies questions. The objective of this activity is to get all students to respond simultaneously and immediately assess students' understanding and retention.

**WHO:**        Early and Middle Grades, High School

**WHEN:**       During a lesson

**THEME(S):**   Time, Continuity, and Change; Culture

- Collect and bring to class artifacts that represent past periods of history. Local museums often have trunks of artifacts that are available for teacher use. Check with a museum in your area. Place the artifacts at various locations around the room and number them. Have students work individually or in pairs taking turns holding and examining the artifacts. Have them guess what each artifact is and what it may have been used for. Have students write their guesses down next to the appropriate number. Once everyone has had an opportunity to examine each artifact, allow them to either confirm or correct their guesses.

**WHO:**        Early and Middle Grades, High School

**WHEN:**       Before and after a lesson

**THEME(S):**   All

- Engage students in the *Sort and Report* activity using the following guidelines: (1) Pick a social studies topic that is about to be studied and on a piece of paper list words and phrases that are connected to it. (2) Have students work with a partner or in groups to cut the words and phrases apart to use as manipulatives. (3) Have students discuss the words and concepts and put them into categories that are then labeled by the group. (4) Have students make predictions about what the social studies topic will be about based on the concepts and categories. (5) Then, have them read the passage or chapter and then revisit the categories. (6) If necessary, have students re-sort the categories based on what they have read. (7) Have student groups create a final sort and provide a reason for why they sorted the categories the way they did (Perez, 2008).

**WHO:**        Early and Middle Grades, High School

**WHEN:**       Before and after a lesson

**THEME(S):**   All

- *Student-Generated Sort and Report* is a variation on the aforementioned activity. The steps are as follows: (1) Have students work together in pairs or small groups to brainstorm original words and phrases that come to mind when they think of a given social studies topic that is to be studied. (2) Have students cut the words and phrases apart to use as manipulatives. (3) Have students work with another group to share their words and categories. (4) Appoint a reporter for each group who remains at the table. The other students become *roving reporters* and visit other tables studying their ideas and labels. (5) Have groups return to their original tables and refine their categories. (6) Each group prepares to discuss any new insights or questions with the whole class. (7) Have students tell what they noticed about their own thinking as they sorted, categorized, and labeled words and phrases related to the topic (Perez, 2008).

**WHO:**        Middle Grades, High School

**WHEN:**       During a lesson

**THEME(S):**   Time, Continuity, and Change

- Lead students in a discussion about the work of an archaeologist, how they focus on human history, and what tools are needed to complete their work. Give each student a chocolate chip cookie and a toothpick. Have students replicate the work of an archaeologist by attempting to remove the chocolate chips from the cookie without destroying the cookie itself. The task will be difficult. Use this activity as a springboard to a discussion on how difficult it must be for an archaeologist to dig for specific historical items while attempting to leave the earth intact.

**WHO:**        Middle Grades, High School

**WHEN:**       After a lesson

**THEME(S):**   All

- Hand out strips of sticky dots to your students and allow a set number of minutes, such as 10 or 12, for them to look through their personal notes taken following a lesson, and highlight, with the dots, major points that they want to remember (Gregory & Herndon, 2010).

**WHO:**        Middle Grades, High School

**WHEN:**       After a lesson

**THEME(S):**   Civic Ideals and Practices

- Have students go on a *good guy/bad guy* hunt through the newspaper or on the Internet trying to find as many examples as possible of someone being a *good citizen* and of someone being a *bad citizen*. Have them work in cooperative groups to cut out their examples, assemble them on a chart, and study them with the goal of coming up with a team definition of *citizenship*. After the group has written down their definition, have them check a dictionary, a textbook, or the Internet for a definition. Have each group compare their personal definition with the definition found. Have them decide if any of their examples would shift on the chart, based on the formal definition of citizenship. Involve students in a whole-class discussion.

**WHO:**        Middle Grades, High School

**WHEN:**      After a lesson

**THEME(S):**   All

- Have students work in cooperative groups of four to six to build models or make maps that will assist them in understanding a social studies concept or location. Students could build models or construct maps that depict the geographical features or population data of local, national, or international locations. Students should be creative as to what materials they would use to construct their models or maps.

**WHO:**        Elementary and Middle Grades, High School

**WHEN:**      After a lesson

**THEME(S):**   All

- As a review activity following a lesson, post four questions pertaining to the lesson around the room, each on a different piece of chart paper. Give each student four sticky notes and have them write their answer to each question on a separate note, get up, and place it on the chart paper under the question. Then have students get up to read the answers from their peers to each of the questions. This activity not only incorporates the strategy of manipulatives by using the sticky notes, but it also integrates the strategies of writing and movement, thereby appealing to more than one modality for students.

**WHO:**        Middle Grades, High School

**WHEN:**      During a lesson

**THEME(S):**   Power, Authority, and Governance

- Have students create hand signals for the seven principles of government and teach those signals to another student. The hand signals will place the principles into one of the strongest memory systems, procedural memory, and make it easier to recall those principles later.

## REFLECTION AND APPLICATION

How will I incorporate *manipulatives, experiments, labs, and models* into instruction to engage students' brains?

*Which manipulatives, experiments, labs, and models am I already incorporating into my social studies curriculum?*

*What additional activities will I incorporate?*

# Metaphors, Analogies, and Similes

## WHAT: DEFINING THE STRATEGY

To understand how limited the resources of the earth are compared with the number of people who have to use them, provide the following demonstration. Have students compare the earth to an apple. Cut the apple into four quarters. Three of those quarters represent the ocean. Name the oceans, eat the three parts and discard the apple. The fourth quarter represents the continents. Name the continents. Now cut the fourth quarter in half ($\frac{1}{8}$ of the apple). This represents inhospitable land. Eat and discard. Now, cut the remaining piece in half ($\frac{1}{16}$ of the apple). This represents land that is too wet, steep, or arid to inhabit for most people. Eat and discard. Now, cut the remaining piece in half ($\frac{1}{32}$ of the apple). This represents land that is not used for one reason or another (too remote, national parks, or open land). Eat and discard. Now with the $\frac{1}{32}$ piece left, peel off the skin. This represents the productive surface that supports more than 6 billion people. It looks, and is, very fragile. It is also the most polluted segment of all of the pieces shown. This is an excellent metaphor for how limited the resources of the earth are and how we must protect our planet (Tate & Phillips, 2011).

The strategy of using metaphors, analogies, and similes is one of the most powerful strategies on the list of 20. If teachers can find a way to take a social studies concept that is unfamiliar to students and compare it to one that is familiar, students' brains stand a better chance of remembering the original concept.

# WHY: THEORETICAL FRAMEWORK

Direct analogy, a basic form of analogy, causes students to become deep thinkers regarding a concept and its characteristics (Gregory & Herndon, 2010).

Older adolescents have an increased ability to understand analogies, metaphors, and symbolism (Feinstein, 2009).

When teaching social studies to English language learners, teachers should create analogies that help them to link the unfamiliar with the familiar (Sousa, 2011).

Metaphors can be useful to shift a student's frame of reference since they use one concept to explain another concept (Caine, Caine, McClintic, & Klimek, 2009).

Metaphors abstract some of the qualities of one concept and apply them in a new context (Caine et al., 2009).

A personal analogy, where a student identifies with an animal, an object, another person, or something else, assists students in analyzing and developing empathy for others (Gregory & Herndon, 2010).

Creating metaphors and creating analogies are two of the four types of tasks that students should use when identifying similarities and developing knowledge (Marzano, 2007).

Analogies can give a teacher insight into a student's inaccuracies and misconceptions about the content and are, therefore, invaluable to teachers (Keeley, 2008).

In a direct analogy, students are told to select a topic that they want to study in detail and then examine how that topic is similar to something else that appears to be quite different (Gregory & Herndon, 2010).

The majority of concepts can be understood but only in relation to other concepts (Lakoff & Johnson, 1980).

# HOW: INSTRUCTIONAL ACTIVITIES

**WHO:**      Early and Middle Grades, High School

**WHEN:**     During a lesson

**THEME(S):**   All

- Since the brain thinks in connections, when possible, introduce a new social studies concept by comparing it to a concept that students already know and understand. When the comparison uses the words *like* or *as*, it is called a simile. Since similes are easier to understand than metaphors, you might want to begin with these. For example, the current economic downturn in the United States is like the Great Depression of the 1930s.

**WHO:**         Middle Grades, High School

**WHEN:**       During a lesson

**THEME(S):**    All

- Metaphors compare two or more ideas without the use of *like* or *as*, and although they are often more difficult to comprehend, they should be used consistently during teaching to make connections between the new social studies concept you want to teach and a concept that your students already know. For example, you could ask students, *Why is America a salad bowl?* The answer would be as follows: *A salad bowl enables ingredients (such as tomatoes, lettuce, onions, carrots, and so forth) to co-exist. Each ingredient keeps its own distinct flavor but if it were not present, the salad would lose some of its overall appeal. This is the case with the diverse groups in America. Each group should be valued for the flavor it adds to American society.*

**WHO:**         Middle Grades, High School

**WHEN:**       During a lesson

**THEME(S):**    All

- Use the pattern a : b :: c : d (a is to b as c is to d) to show how two sets of ideas and concepts are related. For example, Eli Whitney : the cotton gin :: Thomas Edison : the light bulb. Once students are familiar with the concept, have them create their own original analogies, leaving part of the analogy blank so that classmates can complete it.

**WHO:**         Early Grades

**WHEN:**       During a lesson

**THEME(S):**    Individual Development and Identity

- To enable your students to understand themselves and express their emotions, and to assist them in developing empathy for others, have them create personal analogies where they compare themselves to an inanimate object, an animal, or something else. The children's book *I'm as Quick as a Cricket* by Audrey Wood provides excellent examples and illustrations on how those similes can be made. Have students fill in the pattern *I'm as _____ as a _____* and then tell why they are comparing themselves to something else (Gregory & Herndon, 2010).

**WHO:**          Early Grades

**WHEN:**          During a lesson

**THEME(S):**          People, Places, and Environment

- To help students understand the directions of *North, South, East,* and *West,* compare the directions to the numbers on a clock. Show students a visual of a clock and ask them to visualize that they are standing in the middle of the clock facing the number 12. The number 12 represents the direction *North.* If that is the case, the number 6 would represent the direction *South,* the number 3 would represent *East,* and the number 9 would represent *West.* Whenever they forget how the directions relate to one another, remind them of the clock.

**WHO:**          Middle Grades, High School

**WHEN:**          During a lesson

**THEME(S):**          All

- Increase students' analytical thinking by having them simultaneously explore the upside and downside of an idea in social studies, such as *How is the use of technology both a blessing and a curse?* or *how is welfare both a help and a hindrance?* By examining the conflicting viewpoints, have them gain a more in-depth understanding of the concept rather than just examining one point of view. Students can then elaborate on each conflicting viewpoint in writing (Gregory & Herndon, 2010).

**WHO:**          Middle Grades, High School

**WHEN:**          During a lesson

**THEME(S):**          All

- Have students form direct analogies by taking a social studies concept and connecting it to another concept that is quite dissimilar. For example, *How is democracy like a railway station?* or *How is an election like a pizza?* This activity is great for encouraging students to become critical thinkers (Gregory & Herndon, 2010).

**WHO:**          Middle Grades, High School

**WHEN:**          During a lesson

**THEME(S):**          All

- Have students look for examples of metaphors, analogies, and similes in social studies texts and class discussions. Post the list of these examples as a visual in the room and add to it continuously throughout the term. Review the list periodically to facilitate the memories of students.

**WHO:**      Middle Grades, High School

**WHEN:**     During a lesson

**THEME(S):**  All

- To take advantage of the fact that the brain thinks in connections, take two or more social studies concepts that are related to one another and teach them at the same time. For example, teach the concept of immigration when you teach exportation, teach imports when you teach exports, teach democracy, dictatorship, and socialism together, teach Bastille Day when you teach Independence Day. Making connections between concepts facilitates memory and understanding for students.

**WHO:**      Early and Middle Grades, High School

**WHEN:**     During a lesson

**THEME(S):**  All

- Have students use a *peg-word system* to capitalize on the brain's ability to link or connect items together and remember them in order. Have students associate a rhyming word with each number 1 through 10. For example, 1 = bun, 2 = shoe, 3 = tree, 4 = door, 5 = hive, 6 = sticks, 7 = heaven, 8 = gate, 9 = sign, and 10 = hen. Then have them link each item on the list to be remembered with the designated rhyming word in the most absurd visual possible. For example, if the fourth item on the list is the Mississippi River, visualize the Mississippi River flowing up against a door. That will make it easy to remember that the river is the fourth item on the list.

# REFLECTION AND APPLICATION

> How will I incorporate *metaphors, analogies, and similes* into instruction to engage students' brains?

*Which metaphor, analogy, and simile activities am I already incorporating into my social studies curriculum?*

*What additional activities will I incorporate?*

# Strategy 9

# Mnemonic Devices

## WHAT: DEFINING THE STRATEGY

I was asked to teach a social studies lesson recently in a middle school in Texas. By the end of the lesson, students were to know the names of the original 13 colonies and their founders. When planning the lesson, I determined that the use of mnemonic devices would be a great way to help students remember the colonies. I told them the true story that I am from one of the original colonies, Georgia, and that I am a nice person and a great cook. One of my favorite Southern dishes is rice and gravy. Then I taught them to remember the southern colonies with the following mnemonic device: **V**ery **N**ice **S**outherners **M**ake **G**ravy. The first letter in each word in this sentence stands for one of the southern colonies: **V**irginia, **N**orth Carolina, **S**outh Carolina, **M**aryland, and **G**eorgia. This sentence, or acrostic, made it much easier for students to recall the original Southern colonies.

Mnemonic devices derive from the Greek word *mnema*, which means memory, since they are effective ways of helping students and adults remember content. We know that the purpose of social studies instruction is not to have students memorize many isolated facts, but to enable them to have conceptual understanding, but there may be times when they simply need to remember some crucial information. Since the brain is constantly seeking connections, mnemonic devices work because they connect content together either in a word or in a sentence. When the connection is in a word, it is called an acronym. Each letter in the word, or acronym, stands for the concept to be remembered. For example, to remember the Great Lakes, one only needs to recall the word *HOMES—Huron, Ontario, Michigan, Erie,* and *Superior.* When the connection occurs in a sentence, it is called an acrostic. My original mnemonic device for the Southern colonies is considered an acrostic. Either one works well for improving the recall of historical information.

76

## WHY: THEORETICAL FRAMEWORK

The use of acronyms is a common and fun strategy that can be used when students are learning by rote, but younger students do better with auditory mnemonics (Feinstein, 2009).

Mnemonics are more meaningful to adolescents when the students personally create them (Feinstein, 2009).

Acronyms organize information into chunks so students do not need to recall a great deal of information all at one time and also know how many items need to be remembered (Allen, 2008a).

*According to research, people who use mnemonics learn two to three times as much as those who rely on their normal learning habits* (Markowitz & Jensen, 2007, p. 178).

Since mnemonic strategies help students both remember and understand information, they can involve higher level thought processes when appropriately used (Marzano, 2007).

Acrostics work better if the material is familiar since it serves only as a trigger and students still have to recall the original information on which the acrostic is based (Allen, 2008a).

Ordinary people can greatly increase their memory performance, since mnemonic devices can help people recall patterns, rules, or unrelated information (Sousa, 2006).

Mnemonic devices are best used when students have had the opportunity to completely process the information beforehand (Marzano, 2007).

When students have to memorize information that can be arbitrary and dull, mnemonics can be beneficial since they use words and images (Carney & Levin, 2000).

Since the mental capabilities of adolescents are more highly developed, they do well with either visual or auditory mnemonics (Wang & Thomas, 1995).

## HOW: INSTRUCTIONAL ACTIVITIES

**WHO:**       Early and Middle Grades, High School

**WHEN:**      During a lesson

**THEME(S):**  All

- When students have to remember a series of things, create a mnemonic device that will enable them to connect those things together. In the introduction to this chapter, I related an acrostic I created for remembering the Southern colonies. One teacher in my class created the following three acrostics to recall all 13 colonies: for the Southern colonies, she used the acrostic *Mary Never Got to See Vegas* (**M**aryland, **N**orth Carolina, **G**eorgia, **S**outh Carolina, **V**irginia); for the Middle colonies she used *No Dog, No Poop* (**N**ew York, **D**elaware, **N**ew Jersey, **P**ennsylvania); and for the New England Colonies she used *Never Make Raspberry Cupcakes* (**N**ew Hampshire, **M**assachusetts, **R**hode Island, **C**onnecticut).

(Kendra Tollackson, seventh- and eighth-grade Social Studies, Sunnyslope Elementary, Phoenix, AZ)

**WHO:**        Middle Grades and High School

**WHEN:**        During a lesson

**THEME(S):**        All

- When students have to remember a series of things, have them create an original mnemonic device that will enable them to connect those things together. For example, to remember the five states that border the state of Virginia, a student could create the acrostic *Kiss Me With No Teeth*, which stands for *Kentucky, Maryland, West Virginia, North Carolina,* and *Tennessee*.

**WHO:**        Middle Grades and High School

**WHEN:**        During a lesson

**THEME(S):**        Power, Authority, and Governance

- Have students remember the *MAIN* causes of World War I by remembering the acronym *MAIN*. The causes are *Militarism, Alliances, Imperialism,* and *Nationalism*.

(Paul Rizzo, The Pinckney Academy, Moore County Schools, Carthage, NC)

**WHO:**        Early and Middle Grades, High School

**WHEN:**        During a lesson

**THEME(S):**        People, Places, and Environments

- To recall the four oceans of the world, *Indian, Arctic, Atlantic,* and *Pacific*, have students remember the acrostic *I Am A Person* (Feinstein, 2009).

**WHO:**        Middle Grades, High School

**WHEN:**        During a lesson

**THEME(S):**        Power, Authority, and Governance

- To recall the freedoms guaranteed in the first amendment, have students remember the acronym *RAPPS*. The freedoms are *Religion, Assembly, Press, Petition,* and *Speech*.

(Charon L. Williams, Grades 10 Civics, 11 U.S. History, Carver High School, Winston Salem Forsyth County Schools, Winston-Salem, NC)

| | |
|---|---|
| **WHO:** | Middle Grades, High School |
| **WHEN:** | During a lesson |
| **THEME(S):** | Power, Authority, and Governance |

- To recall the five reasons for Imperialism, have students remember the acronym *CREMP*. The reasons are *Cultural, Religious, Economic, Military,* and *Political.*

(Charon L. Williams, Grades 10 Civics, 11 U.S. History, Carver High School, Winston Salem Forsyth County Schools, Winston-Salem, NC)

| | |
|---|---|
| **WHO:** | Middle Grades, High School |
| **WHEN:** | During a lesson |
| **THEME(S):** | Production, Distribution, and Consumption |

- To recall the four factors of Production, have students remember the acronym *CELL*. The four factors are *Capital, Entrepreneur, Land,* and *Labor.*

(Charon L. Williams, Grades 10 Civics, 11 U.S. History, Carver High School, Winston Salem Forsyth County Schools, Winston-Salem, NC)

| | |
|---|---|
| **WHO:** | Middle Grades, High School |
| **WHEN:** | During a lesson |
| **THEME(S):** | All |

- Have students use the *Acrostics Topics* activity to recall pertinent information regarding a social studies topic. Divide students into groups of four to six. Give each group a large piece of chart paper with a topic written horizontally down the left-hand side. This topic will provide an acronym that each group will use to delineate facts about the topic. For example, if the acronym is *COLONIES,* one group's chart could say *Came to America for religious freedom; On long trips in boats; Loyalists agreed with the British King; Often people farmed and hunted; No taxation without representation; If you wanted independence you were a patriot; Even kids helped out with chores like cooking or fishing; Some took the Native Americans' land.* Have groups share their respective finished products with the class. If groups cannot think of a fact that begins with the designated acronym, have them use references such as their textbook or the Internet for assistance. Watch the creativity in students' brains emerge (Green & Casale-Giannola, 2011)!

## REFLECTION AND APPLICATION

> How will I incorporate *mnemonic devices* into instruction to engage students' brains?

*Which mnemonic devices am I already incorporating into my social studies curriculum?*

*What additional devices will I incorporate?*

# Strategy 10

# Movement

## WHAT: DEFINING THE STRATEGY

Teachers have always used the mnemonic device *Never Eat Soggy Waffles* to help students remember their directions, *North, East, South,* and *West.* An even better way to remember them is to do the *Direction Dance.* To perform this dance, you and your students should all stand and face in the same direction with you in front providing a visual. Lead students through the following four steps. Take your right foot and take one step forward, and bring the left foot even with the right while saying the direction word *North.* Take the left foot and take one step backward, and bring the right foot backward even with the left while saying the direction word *South.* Take the right foot and take one step to the right, and bring the left foot over while saying the direction word *East.* Last, take the left foot and take one step to the left, and bring the right foot over while saying the direction word *West.* Repeat these four steps three times and then freeze and turn clockwise. Repeat the same four steps in each direction until you come back to your original position. The *Direction Dance* looks so good when the entire class is doing it together with music. The song *You Should Be Dancing* by the Bee Gee's works very well while doing this dance.

Of all 20 strategies, the strategy of movement is probably my favorite. Not only does it create a fun and motivating atmosphere in the classroom, but it helps to ensure that students will still remember content long after the lesson has been taught. When people are moving, they are putting the information in one of the strongest memory systems, *procedural* or *muscle memory*. This memory system is the reason that people do not forget how to drive a car, ride a bike, play the piano, type, tie their shoes, or brush their teeth. Remember that the person in the classroom who is doing the most work is also growing the most brain cells or dendrites.

## WHY: THEORETICAL FRAMEWORK

Teachers who use movement and kinesthetic learning activities during class and who present information in short intervals can even engage students who have difficulty with attention and hyperactivity (Green & Casale-Giannola, 2011).

Seventeen action research projects all point to the fact that using movement and other kinesthetic activities in the classroom can have the following benefits: preparation of students' brains and bodies for learning; increased student motivation; more positive learning states and classroom environments; increased test scores due to easier recall and retention of information; and increased student participation, attention, and engagement (Lengel & Kuczala, 2010).

Physical activity helps all students deal with stress and can decrease the attention-deficit/hyperactivity disorder student's reliance on medication (Algozzine, Campbell, & Wang, 2009a).

Kinesthetic activities in the classroom were found to create student enthusiasm, assist in increasing benchmark scores, and enhance the total academic experience for eighth grade students (Adams, 2009).

Exercise promotes neurogenesis, or the development of new nerve cells in the brain. It also encourages those nerve cells already in the brain to bond with one another, which forms the basis of new learning (Ratey, 2008).

It is essential that educators incorporate movement into their classrooms since it is thought that at least 85% of students are predominately kinesthetic learners (Lengel & Kuczala, 2010).

Movement can enable teachers to observe the engagement of their students in the lesson and, therefore, assess their understanding of the material (Allen, 2008a).

Reviewing material during the middle of class by using a movement activity has the following benefits: providing students' brains time to rejuvenate and consolidate the new information; improving discipline and student motivation; waking up students' bodies as they begin to tire; and creating a fun, social, and exciting environment in which to learn (Lengel & Kuczala, 2010).

When students sit too long in class, their natural processes begin to shut down: blood settles in their buttocks and feet and less oxygen is able to get to their brains. Neither of these reactions supports learning (Allen, 2008a).

Keeping students from moving in class may be the one most significant impediment to their learning and ability to recall new information (Jensen, 2002).

# HOW: INSTRUCTIONAL ACTIVITIES

**WHO:**        Early and Middle Grades, High School

**WHEN:**       During a lesson

**THEME(S):**   All

- Remember the formula (*AS = age*) to recall the average attention span of a student. In this formula, the *AS* is a mnemonic device for *Attention Span*. The average attention span of a student is equal to their age in minutes. Therefore, the attention span of a 7-year-old is 7 minutes, for a 12-year-old it would be 12 minutes, and for a 16-year-old it would be 16 minutes. For example, a 15-year old sitting in a 90-minute block of instructional time should have approximately six different changes of activity since the average attention span would be 15 minutes.

**WHO:**        Early and Middle Grades, High School

**WHEN:**       During a lesson

**THEME(S):**   All

- When a student provides an answer for the class, have the other students stand (instead of raising their hands) if they agree with the answer and remain seated if they disagree. Standing can supply additional blood and oxygen throughout the body and assist students in remaining more alert.

**WHO:**        Early and Middle Grades, High School

**WHEN:**       During a lesson

**THEME(S):**   All

- Have students draw the seasonal cycle below. Put on some fast-paced music and have them walk around the room making appointments with one classmate for each season. Have them write the name of each classmate on the appropriate line. When it becomes necessary for one student to talk to another regarding something that is being taught in class or to reteach a concept previously taught, have them keep one of their four seasonal appointments. One seasonal cycle may last for several days depending on how often students need to keep an appointment.

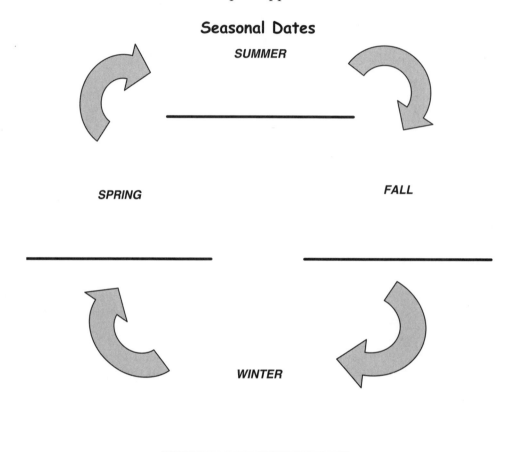

**Seasonal Dates**

SUMMER

SPRING

FALL

WINTER

Adaptation: Rather than keeping a seasonal appointment in social studies class, have students make and keep appointments with classmates using the historical time line below.

## Appointment Time Line

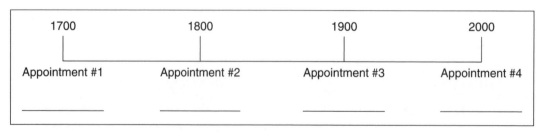

| 1700 | 1800 | 1900 | 2000 |
|------|------|------|------|
| Appointment #1 | Appointment #2 | Appointment #3 | Appointment #4 |

**WHO:**        Early and Middle Grades, High School

**WHEN:**        During a lesson

**THEME(S):**    All

- Have students look around the room until they *lock eyes* with another student. This student becomes their *energizing partner*. Anytime during the class period when a question needs to be discussed or a concept retaught, have students stand up and meet with their *energizing partner*. Any student who does not have a partner should meet at a designated place in the room. Pair those who do not have partners together. *Energizing partners* are constantly changing so that students are not always meeting with the same students.

**WHO:**        Early and Middle Grades, High School

**WHEN:**       During a lesson

**THEME(S):**   All

- Engage students by having them stand and chorally read a specific passage from the social studies textbook or answer a specific question. The fun of this activity is increased when students read with a specific accent, without taking a breath, while standing on one foot, or while holding their paper in the air or upside down.

**WHO:**        Early and Middle Grades, High School

**WHEN:**       During a lesson

**THEME(S):**   All

- Post pictures or readings around the room. Periodically give students assignments that require that they get up from their desk and look at the pictures or read the readings around the room to answer designated questions. During a test, you could even put the test questions in different baskets around the room and have students get up and select a question, take it back to their desks, and respond to it in writing. When the responses are completed, students would then put the questions back in the appropriate baskets and proceed to other baskets with additional questions.

**WHO:**        Early and Middle Grades, High School

**WHEN:**       During a lesson

**THEME(S):**   All

- Put on some fast-paced, high-energy music. Have students put their pens and papers down, stand up, and walk around the room until you stop the music. Tell them to *put some pep in their step*. When the music stops, have them pair with someone standing close to them and discuss the answer to a designated social studies question or reteach a concept you have just taught. After 1 to 2 minutes of conversation, start the music again, have students walk in a different direction, and repeat the procedure with a different partner and a different task.

**WHO:**     Early and Middle Grades, High School

**WHEN:**     During a lesson

**THEME(S):**     All

- Engage students in a *carousel gallery walk*. Set up four easels or four pieces of chart paper on the wall in four different places in the room. Write a different social studies question or idea to comment about on each piece of paper. Place students in four groups and have them rotate to each easel and answer the question or respond to the idea. Have each group appoint a scribe who writes the group's answer on the paper. Adding some high-energy music to this task will heighten its appeal to students.

**WHO:**     Early and Middle Grades, High School

**WHEN:**     Before, during, or after a lesson

**THEME(S):**     All

- Put up a *Parking Lot* in your social studies classroom. A *Parking Lot* consist of one piece of chart paper on the wall with the words *Parking Lot* written on it and four colored, medium-size sticky notes adhered to it. (See the diagram below.) At any time that direct instruction is not occurring, students can get up, go to the *Parking Lot,* and take a sticky note back to their desks. They can write any question they may have about the lesson on the sticky note. Students do not have to put their names on the note. They then get up and stick the note back in the *Parking Lot.* Keep an eye on the *Parking Lot* throughout the day or period and when you see a question, answer it for the whole class. This not only provides some movement for students, but it gives students an opportunity to ask questions that they may not feel comfortable asking aloud in class. Any inappropriate questions should be ignored.

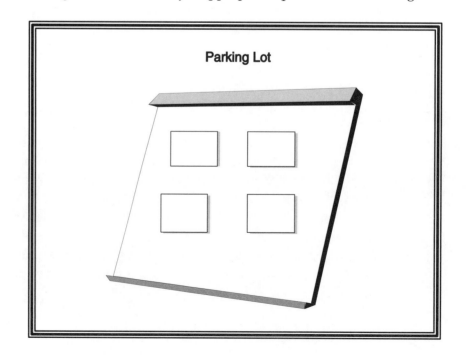

**WHO:**          Early Grades

**WHEN:**         During a lesson

**THEME(S):**     Individual Development and Identity

- Give each student a partner. Have them stand and talk with their partner to find out how they may be alike and how they may be different. Have them discuss likes and dislikes, talents, strengths or things they do well, favorite activities, favorite school subjects, pet peeves or dislikes, and so forth. Following a 3- to 5-minute conversation, have them sit down and complete a Venn diagram that shows ways that they are alike and different from their partner. Use this activity as a lead-in to a discussion regarding how we perceive and are perceived by others.

**WHO:**          Early and Middle Grades

**WHEN:**         During a lesson

**THEME(S):**     Power, Authority, and Governance

- When teaching the branches of the federal government, make three signs (*Executive, Legislative,* and *Judicial*) and place them on the wall in three different places in the room. Teach students about the branches, the function of each, and what positions are in what branch. The graphic organizer in the beginning of Chapter 5 can be used to facilitate this discussion. Then move around the classroom and *anoint* students with power. I have a magic wand for the anointing that students absolutely love. It lights up and makes a noise when you push a button. For example, put the wand on the shoulder of a student and say, *You are a Supreme Court Justice. Go stand in the branch where you belong.* The student should then get up and stand under the sign that says *Judicial* branch. Assign each student a governmental role, and have them get up and move to the appropriate branch. Once every student is standing in a branch, ask the students one by one what their position is. Have the class determine if they moved to the correct branch. I actually used this lesson with one class and when I left, everyone in there, including special education students, knew the branches of the federal government and who was in what branch. The movement went a long way toward accomplishing this objective!

**WHO:**          Middle Grades, High School

**WHEN:**         During a lesson

**THEME(S):**     Time, Continuity, and Change

- Create a living time line by writing 5 to 10 different historical events on index cards. Pass each card out randomly to a student in class. Have students with cards come to the front of the room and hold their cards up for the remainder of the class to see. Have a student come to the front of the class and move classmates with cards around until each of the events is in chronological order from oldest to most recent. Have the remainder of the class determine if the placement is accurate. To make the activity more challenging, have the student place the living time line in order before a short song ends. I have used the theme from the game show *The Price Is Right* as the song. It lasts about 2 minutes.

**WHO:**          Middle Grades, High School

**WHEN:**        During a lesson

**THEME(S):**    People, Places, and Environment

- Use the tiles on the floor or ceiling of the classroom as lines of latitude and longitude. Start by giving students a general location; the tile in the center of the room represents 100 degrees latitude, for example, or a specific point in the room is Australia. Have students take turns getting up and moving to specific locations, such as the continents, oceans, equator, prime meridian, and specific countries. Allow other students to challenge the location that each student selects and let them debate where the exact location in the classroom would be.

**WHO:**          High School

**WHEN:**        During a lesson

**THEME(S):**    Production, Distribution, and Consumption

- Make 30 flash cards with a number on one side and the sentences below on the other. You will also need a ball of string. Hand one card out randomly to each student. Have students stand and form a large circle. Beginning with card #1, have each student read the information aloud. For example, the student who has card #1 will say, *Libya sells oil to Norway.* Have that student hold the beginning of the string. The string then goes to the person holding the card whose country receives the goods. Therefore, in the example, the student who gets the string next would be the student holding card #4, *Norway sells fish to Sweden.* Continue until all cards have been read. The string will resemble a spider web with each student holding a corner. Once all cards have been read, ask the following questions:

  o What if there was a trade embargo on food? All those who sold food to another country, pull tight on your string. How many can feel that?
  o What if a hostile country took over a country where most of the world's oil supply was found? All those who sold oil to another country, pull tight on your string. How many can feel that?
  o What if all the countries who sold machinery got together and decided to keep it for themselves? All those who sold machinery to another country, pull tight on your string. How many can feel that?
  o Help students understand how dependent we truly are on one another.

| | |
|---|---|
| 1. Libya sells oil to Norway. | 16. Switzerland sells watches to Albania. |
| 2. Afghanistan sells dried fruit to Libya. | 17. Portugal sells cork to Britain. |
| 3. Sweden sells wood to Germany. | 18. Greece sells tobacco to Portugal. |
| 4. Norway sells fish to Sweden. | 19. The Netherlands sells chocolate to Japan. |
| 5. Germany sells machinery to France. | 20. Britain sells manufactured goods to the Netherlands. |
| 6. Italy sells footwear to the USA. | 21. Algeria sells wine to Austria. |
| 7. France sells textiles to Italy. | 22. Japan sells machinery to Hong Kong. |
| 8. The USA sells machinery to Canada. | 23. Hong Kong sells manufactured goods to Algeria. |
| 9. Venezuela sells gold to Brazil. | 24. Austria sells coal to Argentina. |
| 10. Canada sells wheat to Venezuela. | 25. Bahrain sells oil to Australia. |
| 11. Brazil sells coffee to Djibouti. | 26. Argentina sells wheat to Cuba. |
| 12. Djibouti sells hides to Somalia. | 27. Cuba sells sugar to The United Arab Emirates. |
| 13. Somalia sells food to Saudi Arabia. | 28. Angola sells coffee to Bahrain. |
| 14. Saudi Arabia sells oil to Switzerland. | 29. The United Arab Emirates sells oil to Angola. |
| 15. Albania sells wheat to Greece. | 30. Australia sells wheat to Afghanistan. |

## REFLECTION AND APPLICATION

How will I incorporate *movement* into
instruction to engage students' brains?

**Which movement activities am I already incorporating into my social studies curriculum?**

**What additional activities will I incorporate?**

# Strategy 11

# Music, Rhythm, Rhyme, and Rap

## WHAT: DEFINING THE STRATEGY

*Schoolhouse Rock* had the right idea more than 30 years ago. By watching cartoon characters and singing along on Saturday mornings, we learned the *Preamble to the Constitution* and realized how a bill became a law. I know you recall *I'm just a bill up on Capitol Hill. . . .* Recently in one of my classes, a participant shared that she has a Korean friend who is studying for American citizenship. She is actually watching old episodes of *Schoolhouse Rock* and it is really helping her remember more and more of what she needs to know about this country.

In another book, I related this true story but it bears repeating since this is a social studies book. A Navy sailor named Douglas Hegdahl was captured during the Vietnam War and taken to the Hanoi Hilton, which was a prisoner-of-war (POW) camp. Since Douglas was going to be released eventually, the military wanted him to remember the names of as many POWs as possible so that their families could be notified. They had Douglas sing the names to the tune of *Old MacDonald Had a Farm*. When he was eventually released, he sang the names of 256 POWs to that tune. Even the military knows the power of music!

Social studies teachers are still using music as a teaching tool. When students have to memorize content or when you want to be sure that they can synthesize what you have taught into another form, have them convert it to music. It will surely pay off! Music also helps you create an optimal mood for learning in your social studies classroom.

# WHY: THEORETICAL FRAMEWORK

Various forms of musical expression, such as listening, singing, dancing, and playing an instrument, can add memorable and meaningful first-hand experiences to a social studies classroom (Parker, 2009).

Studies at Brigham Young University suggest that music is best played when students are practicing math problems, doing art work, and writing, and during the opening of class, but should probably not be used when directions are being given or during silent reading (Delandtsheer, 2011).

The type of music should be matched to the teachable tasks. For example, classical music from the baroque period or mellow New Age music can be used during seat work, rhythm and blues for fun times, high-tempo for fast-paced movement, upbeat New Age for conversational work, oldies for sing-alongs or to accomplish tasks, or appropriate themes from television shows such as the theme from *Jeopardy!* when playing the game (Jensen, 2009).

The use of music will help facilitate students' abilities to learn about and appreciate people and cultures from other countries (Burton & McFarland, 2009).

The use of music in the classroom has the following advantages: it boosts achievement and creativity, embeds the learning faster and deeper, relaxes the brain following stress, calms the hyperactive student, brings the entire group together and motivates them, and simply lets students have fun (Jensen, 2009).

A country's culture, history, and geography can be revealed to students through that country's music (Melber & Hunter, 2010).

Music activates different parts of the brain dependent on the learning tasks. For example, harmony and rhythm activate more of the left brain, melody activates more of the right brain, while the cerebellum is activated by measuring beats (Jensen, 2008).

Teachers should use music to set a mood in the classroom, change the states of students' brains, and create a positive learning environment (Perez, 2008).

When adolescents are actively involved with music, memory, self-esteem, and visual-spatial relations are improved (Kluball, 2000).

Teenagers who are musicians are less, not more, likely to engage in at-risk activities such as using drugs (Costa-Giomi, 1998).

When students listen to music from various cultures, they begin to understand people who live thousands of miles from them or who lived thousands of years ago (Selwyn, 1993).

# HOW: INSTRUCTIONAL ACTIVITIES

**WHO:**       Early and Middle Grades, High School

**WHEN:**      Before or during a lesson

**THEME(S):**    All

- Have calming music playing when students enter your social studies classroom. Music with approximate beats of 50 to 70 per minute can synchronize with the heart and calm the brain down. I know you have heard the expression *Music Hath Charms to Soothe the Savage Beast!* Types of music that fall into this category include classical (particularly from the Baroque period), smooth jazz, New Age (such as Enya or Yani), slow Celtic or Irish music, Native American music, and nature sounds. This type of music can put the brain in the right state for learning.

**WHO:**       Early and Middle Grades, High School

**WHEN:**      Before, during, or after a lesson

**THEME(S):**    All

- High-energy music, or music with approximately 110 to 160 beats per minute, can have a motivating and energizing effect on the brains of your students. Types of music that fall into this category include rhythm and blues, rock and roll, salsa, and fast-paced country and can be integrated into the lesson or played during transition times.

**WHO:**       Early and Middle Grades, High School

**WHEN:**      Before, during, or after a lesson

**THEME(S):**    Culture

- Expose students to the wide variety of music representative of America's diverse cultures. Have each student bring to class one sample of his or her favorite music. Be sure to tell students that the lyrics cannot be objectionable (no profanity or lyrics degrading to other people). Play a sampling of the various types of music for the class and lead the class in a discussion of how the particular music reflects the values of America's culture. If you have students from a variety of cultures, this is a wonderful opportunity for them to showcase the diversity inherent in the particular music of those cultures. Consult the American Jukebox collection at the Library of Congress. The selections of music are in the public domain and one collection spans American history.

**WHO:**       Early and Middle Grades, High School

**WHEN:**      Before, during, or after a lesson

**THEME(S):**    Culture

- One way a country's culture is reflected is in its music. As students study a particular culture, have them analyze the accompanying music of that culture in an effort to understand the diverse perspectives of the people who reside in that culture. Have them compare and contrast these perspectives from those of the types of music heard in mainstream America.

**WHO:**        Early and Middle Grades, High School

**WHEN:**       During a lesson

**THEME(S):**   All

- When students need to learn lists of social studies concepts such as *Presidents of the United States* or *U.S. States and Capitals*, use music. Anything a person puts to music is easier to remember. Teachers relate to me that their students have a difficult time remembering concepts, but those same students are able to walk down the hall singing the lyrics to every song or rap that happens to come on the radio. The company *Rocknlearn* uses rock, rap, and country music to teach concepts. Many of those concepts are in the area of social studies. The CDs come packaged with a book and can be found at a local teacher store or by logging on to www.rocknlearn.com.

**WHO:**        Early and Middle Grades, High School

**WHEN:**       Before and during a lesson

**THEME(S):**   All

- You are more creative than you think! Try your hand at writing an original song, rhyme, or rap, which will help your students remember a social studies concept previously taught. Perform your creative effort for your students and then provide them with a visual and teach it to them. Have them teach it to one another. You will instantly become their favorite teacher, if you are not already!

**WHO:**        Early and Middle Grades, High School

**WHEN:**       During a lesson

**THEME(S):**   All

- As you engage students in playing games such as *Jeopardy!*, *Family Feud*, or *Password*, use the accompanying music to increase interest and create the mood of an actual game show. More than 15 game show themes can be found on the CD *Classic TV Game Show Themes*. Watch how much fun reviewing or introducing social studies content can be when it occurs within the context of a game.

**WHO:**        Early and Middle Grades, High School

**WHEN:**       During a lesson

**THEME(S):**   All

- Many songs actually reflect events in specific periods of history. Find music that relates to the content you are teaching and integrate the songs into your lesson. For example, it was only recently that I learned that the rhyme *Ring Around the Rosie, A Pocket Full of Posies* actually referred to the *Black Plague* since people put posies in their pockets to counteract the stench coming from those who had died of the disease. Two additional examples are as follows: (1) Have students listen to *The Battle of New Orleans* and then describe how the battle was fought. (2) Have students listen to the song *Carefully Taught* from South Pacific as an analogy to where racism originates.

**WHO:**       Early and Middle Grades, High School

**WHEN:**      Before, during, or after a lesson

**THEME(S):**   All

- Since music can literally change the state of students' brains, consult books that will help you select the appropriate type of music for the state you wish to create. Eric Jensen's *Top Tunes for Teaching* or Rich Allen's *The Ultimate Book of Music for Learning* are two of my favorite books for categorizing musical selections according to states of the brain. By the way, the selections work when teaching students or adults!

**WHO:**       Middle Grades, High School

**WHEN:**      During or after a lesson

**THEME(S):**   All

- Have students change the lyrics to a popular song to show their mastery of social studies content. Students can use *www.flocabulary.com* for background beats if they would like to create a rap. Students with access to technology can create a video that accompanies the song. This can be done with something as simple as a student's cell phone or PowerPoint. There is also other free online video creation software, such as *Moviemaker.*

**WHO:**       Middle Grades, High School

**WHEN:**      During or after a lesson

**THEME(S):**   All

- After instructing your students in a major social studies concept, have them write an original song, rhyme, or rap to show their understanding of the concept. Since there may not be enough time in class for this activity, assign it for homework. Give students several nights to complete their creative effort. Then on a designated day, engage the class in a *Talent Show* where students volunteer to appear on *American History Idol* rather than *American Idol*. Have them perform for the class. When students are taking content and putting it in a new form such as a song, rhyme, or rap, they are using one of the highest order thinking skills, known as synthesis.

# REFLECTION AND APPLICATION

How will I incorporate *music, rhythm, rhyme, and rap* into instruction to engage students' brains?

**Which music, rhythm, rhyme, and rap activities am I already incorporating into my social studies curriculum?**

**What additional activities will I incorporate?**

# Strategy 12

# Project-Based and Problem-Based Instruction

## WHAT: DEFINING THE STRATEGY

When my daughter Jessica was in fifth grade, she was assigned a social studies project that she still remembers even though she is almost 30. At the culmination of a unit of study on the Civil War, instead of an objective test, students' knowledge of the content was assessed via a project. The project involved creating a Civil War newspaper. Jessica received a checklist that detailed what the newspaper had to contain. The checklist included the following: a name for the paper, the cost, a slogan, an index, a feature story with an accompanying visual, an advertisement, a crime story, and so forth.

Jessica started work on the project right away and appeared excited about the possibilities. When finished, she shared her project with me before she turned it in to her teacher. The name of her paper was the *J. T. News* (for Jessica Tate News). The cost was a nickel. Her slogan was particularly creative. It was *If you don't get the news from us, you don't get it!* The feature story was about the assassination of the president, Abraham Lincoln. Since Jesse needed an accompanying visual and this occurred before the days of the Internet, she cut Lincoln's picture out of the encyclopedia. (We had a talk about that!) Her advertisement was for horseshoes and her crime story dealt with the fact that John Wilkes Booth was suspected of being the shooter of the president.

Jessica's newspaper received an *A*, but, more important, she not only demonstrated her understanding of Civil War events but also learned the real-world skill of putting together a newspaper. This is what can result when multiple content areas are integrated into completing real-world projects or solving real-world problems.

---

## WHY: THEORETICAL FRAMEWORK

Project-based instruction includes conducting interviews since oral histories can provide students with rich data about the past experiences of diverse populations (Melber & Hunter, 2010).

Idea projects (those that focus on new ideas or take information and use it for another purpose) and presentation projects (those that gather information and present it in a unique way) are two types of projects in which to engage students (Delandtsheer, 2011).

Teachers are building the problem-solving skills advocated by the national standards for social studies when they are creating opportunities for students to observe, make inferences, and share what they have discovered with classmates (Melber & Hunter, 2010).

Active thinking is promoted on the part of students when they work collaboratively to find answers in a problem-based learning approach (Goodnough, 2006).

When students are solving problems, their brains attempt to find connections and patterns and to make sense of the dissonance they are sensing in the problem (Fogarty, 2009).

When students participate in inquiry-based, problem-solving activities, they have the chance to control their own learning (Canestrari, 2005).

*The more complex the problem, the more complex the brain activity becomes* (Fogarty, 2009, p. 154).

Problem-solving strategies that incorporate students' interests apply to all grade levels and content areas, maintain student involvement, and make the learning meaningful (Algozzine, Campbell, & Wang, 2009b).

There is no limit to the type, number, and scope of projects that can be used at the beginning or culmination of a unit of study (Fogarty, 2009).

---

## HOW: INSTRUCTIONAL ACTIVITIES

**WHO:**        Early and Middle Grades, High School

**WHEN:**       During and after a lesson

**THEME(S):**   All

- The procedure below should be followed when engaging students in problem-based learning:

1. Introduce a real-world problem to the class. Discuss it.

2. Have students work together to determine what information is already known and what information needs to be gathered.

3. Have students generate a problem statement.

4. Have them identify solutions that might work.

5. Have them research and analyze solutions.

6. Have them present solutions to the class with documentation to support the solutions.

(National Council for the Social Studies, 2010)

**WHO:**         Early Grades

**WHEN:**        Before a lesson

**THEME(S):**    Individual Development and Identity

- Have students find photos of themselves from birth to the present day that reflect how their individual identity has formed and changed over their life span. Have them create a collage of the photos on a poster and prepare to discuss with the class how the photos reflect the individual changes in looks and personality.

**WHO:**         Middle Grades, High School

**WHEN:**        During a lesson

**THEME(S):**    Culture

- Place students in cooperative groups of four to six. Assign each group a different world culture to research. Students should examine the behaviors, beliefs, traditions, values, institutions, and ways of living together of the particular culture to which they have been assigned. Have them present this information to the class in a creative way, such as a role play or PowerPoint presentation. A graphic organizer similar to the one below could help the group in summarizing and presenting the information. Following all of the presentations, guide students in comparing and contrasting the cultures presented.

| World Culture | |
| --- | --- |
| Behaviors | |
| Beliefs | |
| Traditions | |
| Values | |
| Institutions | |
| Ways of Living | |

**WHO:**       High School

**WHEN:**      After a lesson

**THEME(S):**  Culture; Individual Development and Identity

- Interviews are wonderful ways for students to develop their abilities to think historically. Have them interview members of a subculture such as a community group, an ethnic group, a religious group, or a workplace group on an issue of importance. You may want to role play how to conduct an interview in class prior to students conducting their actual interviews. Based on the information gleaned from the interview, have students write an editorial to the local newspaper that presents the subculture's point of view regarding the issue. I will never forget a graduate class assignment during which I had to interview a family member. I chose my mother. I tape-recorded the interview and later transcribed it. I now have a written history of my mother's life. There were things that I found out about the history of my family that I would never have known had I not completed this assignment.

**WHO:**       Middle Grades, High School

**WHEN:**      After a lesson

**THEME(S):**  Individuals, Groups, and Institutions

- Have students work in pairs to contribute to a class *Wax Museum* by selecting someone of historical significance and researching their life and contributions to society. When the museum is presented, one student dresses up as the historical figure and poses in a perfectly still position as if they were a wax figure while another student narrates about the life of the figure. Students from other classes can come and take a tour through the museum, or it can be presented to the parents and community on a given night.

**WHO:**       High School

**WHEN:**      During a lesson

**THEME(S):**  All

- Present a real-life problem, such as the one described below, to students. Put them into cooperative groups and have them research and brainstorm their options in solving the problem. Create a stack of cards that have answers/responses to the problem and have students work through the situations in their groups. Be sure that you have researched the problem so that the response cards are accurate. Create enough cards so that all groups have to respond to several of them before a final solution is reached.

## Sample Problem

A new family buys and moves into the house next door to you. The family has many dogs, and you notice that the dogs have litters of puppies very frequently. All day and night you hear the dogs barking and howling nonstop. The smell of the dogs also becomes very pronounced. You live far out in a rural area where there is no animal control. What do you do?

**WHO:**   High School

**WHEN:**   During a lesson

**THEME(S):**   People, Places, and Environments

- Have students work individually or in cooperative groups of four to six to create maps that represent changes over a period of time in the borders of a region. Have them glean information from charts, graphs, atlases, databases, and so forth to assist in the creation of their maps (National Council for the Social Studies, 2010).

**WHO:**   Middle Grades, High School

**WHEN:**   During a lesson

**THEME(S):**   People, Places, and Environments

- Have students work individually or in cooperative groups of four to six to graph patterns of human migration in a specific place on the globe for a specified period of time.

**WHO:**   Middle Grades, High School

**WHEN:**   During a lesson

**THEME(S):**   Global Connections

- Have students work in cooperative groups of four to six to complete a project or presentation on a global problem, such as spiraling gasoline prices. Have them state the problem and research possible solutions to the problem. After considering the pros and cons of all of the options, have them create and present a written plan for solving the global problem to the class.

**WHO:**   Early and Middle Grades, High School

**WHEN:**   During and after a lesson

**THEME(S):**   People, Places, and Environments

- When students are complacent about overconsumption, energy efficiency, and saving the planet, try this weeklong project. Allow a group of students to eat lunch in the classroom rather than the cafeteria for one week. Collect the trash from their lunches for the entire week. Show the trash to the class as a visual and lead them in a discussion regarding the impact on the environment if we multiplied this amount of trash from one meal per day times the number of citizens in a city, state, country, or continent. (Darlene Matthews, SPED, Millbrook High School, Raleigh, NC)

WHO:          High School

WHEN:          During a lesson

THEME(S):          Production, Distribution, and Consumption

- Give students different amounts of fictional money ranging from $1,000 to $500,000 and have them buy and sell stocks for a period of 6 weeks. Have students keep a log of each time they buy or sell a stock and the reason behind their actions. Each trade should cost $25.00. At the end of the 6-week period, have students discuss with one another how they made or lost money.

**WHO:**          Middle Grades, High School

**WHEN:**          During a lesson

**THEME(S):**          Power, Authority, and Governance

- Have students work in teams to pick a political party and research the party's social, political, economic, and cultural platforms. Then have them create a fictional candidate that exemplifies the perfect candidate for the party. Have each group create posters, bumper stickers, and radio and television commercials in support of their candidate.

**WHO:**          Middle Grades, High School

**WHEN:**          During a lesson

**THEME(S):**          People, Places, and Environments

- Have students work in cooperative groups of four to six to create a social studies news broadcast for television. This interdisciplinary project should not only integrate the content area of social studies as students research timely, newsworthy topics to be included in the broadcast; it should also integrate English as students write the copy to be delivered by the anchorpersons and practice their public-speaking skills while delivering the actual broadcast. The news broadcast should be presented to the class and evaluated according to a rubric that the class as a whole can help develop.

# REFLECTION AND APPLICATION

How will I incorporate *project-based and problem-based instruction* to engage students' brains?

**Which project-based and problem-based activities am I already incorporating into my social studies curriculum?**

**What additional activities will I incorporate?**

# Strategy 13

# Reciprocal Teaching and Cooperative Learning

## WHAT: DEFINING THE STRATEGY

There may be times in your social studies classroom when it becomes necessary for students to comprehend a great deal of content. When this occurs, the cooperative learning activity called *Jigsaw* might prove helpful. Take the content and divide it into sections of approximately equal length. Place students in cooperative groups. The number of students in each group is determined by the number of sections to be read. Rather than you teaching the content to the entire class, have one student in each group become responsible for teaching one section of the content to the cooperative group. The reason that the activity is called *Jigsaw* is because each student has a piece of the puzzle and, once all the teaching is completed, so is the puzzle.

To engage in *Jigsaw*, have students complete the following steps: (1) Each student reads his or her content silently for the purpose of teaching the most important concepts to the group. Students are encouraged to become experts on their section and to use brain-compatible strategies that make the teaching unforgettable. These could include the use of visuals, graphic organizers, storytelling, or role play. This preparation could be done as homework if time does not permit during class time. (2) Students who have the same section from each group get together and determine what the major points should be and share how they have decided to teach them to their respective groups. (3) Students then return to their original group and are given a predetermined number of minutes to teach the content. (4) After each section has been taught, it is the teacher's job to reiterate the most crucial points so that all students hear the content twice, once from their peers and once from you.

Jigsaw is just one of many ways that students can benefit from working together and teaching one another. Additional ways are outlined in the remainder of this chapter.

## WHY: THEORETICAL FRAMEWORK

*The brains of healthy humans are wired to be social and to connect* (Hyerle & Alper, 2011, p. 31).

When practiced correctly, cooperative learning has an effect that is equivalent to an increase in 27 percentile points for students (Tileston, 2011).

When students work in small groups, true learning takes place since students are able to exchange ideas, get across their points of view, defend the way they think, and probe the way others in the group think (Gregory & Herndon, 2010).

Reciprocal teaching paired with targeted questioning are effective strategies for English language development and increased reading comprehension among English language students (Calderon, 2007).

*Cooperative learning makes thinking and learning audible* (Fogarty, 2009, p. 112).

Peer tutoring enables students to remain focused on a learning activity while interacting with their peers, boosts students' self-esteem, and is an effective way of matching students with similar ability levels and learning disabilities (Algozzine, Campbell, & Wang, 2009a).

Active conversations with other students foster thinking and increase understanding for the listener and the learner (Fogarty, 2009).

Peer tutoring has been recommended as one instructional procedure that decreases the time that teachers have to spend and increases the amount of instructional time with learning-disabled students (Saenz, Fuchs, & Fuchs, 2005).

Cooperative learning groups are characterized by the following five elements: (1) The members are positively interdependent on one another; (2) there is an abundance of face-to-face interaction; (3) each person is individually accountable for the group's goals; (4) interpersonal and small-group skills are frequently practiced; and (5) groups are provided time to process how well they functioned and to improve future effectiveness (Johnson & Johnson, 1994).

Cooperative learning can result in higher achievement and self-esteem, increased collaborative skills and intrinsic motivation, and improved time-on-task as well as better attitudes toward school and teachers (Johnson & Johnson, 1994).

People learn . . .

    10% of what they read

    20% of that they hear

    30% of what they see

    50% of what they both see and hear

    70% of what they say as they talk

    80% of what they experience; and

    95% of what they teach to someone else

                        (Ekwall & Shanker, 1988)

*It is one thing for a student to know information; it is another dimension to be able to explain that information to someone else* (Tileston, 2011).

Although reading, writing, and mathematics are important to a person's success in the workplace, one of the most important skills a teacher can equip a student with is the ability to work with others (Secretary's Commission on Achieving Necessary Skills, 1991).

# HOW: INSTRUCTIONAL ACTIVITIES

**WHO:**        Early and Middle Grades, High School

**WHEN:**      During a lesson

**THEME(S):**    All

- In a brain-compatible classroom, there should be a great deal of student talk. In fact, the person doing the most talking about social studies content is growing the most dendrites, or brain cells. You will not want to waste a minute of class time trying to get the attention of your students when you need it. Create a signal for this purpose. The signal can be a raised hand, a chime, a doorbell, a rain stick, or any other soothing sound. Practice having students get quiet immediately when they hear the sound or see the signal. This way you will not waste one minute of your social studies instructional time trying to get their attention.

**WHO:**        Early and Middle Grades, High School

**WHEN:**      During a lesson

**THEME(S):**    All

- Have each student select a peer or close partner (CP) who sits so close to the student that he or she can talk to this person whenever necessary and not have to move from the desk. As you teach, allow time for students to reteach a chunk of information to their close partner, discuss or brainstorm ideas, or review content prior to testing. Close partners can also answer questions or re-explain a concept that is unclear. The CP activity works well when student talk time is limited.

**WHO:**          Early and Middle Grades, High School

**WHEN:**         During a lesson

**THEME(S):**     All

- *Think, Pair, Share.* Have students *think* about a question related to a social studies concept being taught. Students can even write down their response. Then have them *pair* with another student and discuss their response. If the response is different, students can defend their answer. Last, students are asked to *share* what they discussed with their partner with the remainder of the class. This technique helps to ensure that students who are reluctant to share answers with the class have an opportunity to dialogue answers before they are called upon by the teacher.

**WHO:**          Early and Middle Grades, High School

**WHEN:**         During a lesson

**THEME(S):**     All

- Since the brain has a need to belong, have students work together in *families*, or cooperative groups of four to six students. Students could be seated together in groups or taught to arrange their desks into groups when there is a cooperative learning activity and to place them back once the activity has ended. Groups should probably be of mixed ability levels to take advantage of the multiple intelligences or talents that students display. Groups can even come up with a name, slogan, and cheer to encourage positive interdependence.

**WHO:**          Early and Middle Grades, High School

**WHEN:**         During a lesson

**THEME(S):**     All

- Students do not always come equipped with the social skills necessary for effectively functioning as a cooperative group. When this occurs, you will want to teach students some necessary skills. For example, draw a *T-chart* similar to the one below to delineate what a social skill looks like and what it sounds like. Social skills could include the following: paying attention, critiquing a peer's ideas, encouraging one another.

## Paying Attention

| Looks Like | Sounds Like |
|---|---|
| Eye contact with the speaker | Only one person speaking at a time |
| Leaning forward | Other group members quiet |
| One person speaking | |
| No distractions | |

During a cooperative learning activity, observe each group and make a tally mark on a sheet every time the particular social skill, such as *paying attention*, is practiced by any student in the group. Take time, following the activity to provide feedback to the class. A student may also be assigned to fulfill the function of a *process observer* who does not participate in the activity, but instead collects data for each member in the group and then provides feedback to the group once the activity is over. You may want to make the most talkative student in each group the *process observer* since the person who fulfills that role is not allowed to speak and other students may finally be able to get engaged in the conversation.

**WHO:**      Early and Middle Grades, High School

**WHEN:**      During a lesson

**THEME(S):**      All

- One way to keep all students engaged in a cooperative group activity and to encourage individual accountability is to assign roles for students to fulfill in the group. Some of the following roles can be assigned:

  o **Facilitator:** This CEO of the group ensures that the task is completed and that all students have opportunities to participate.
  o **Scribe:** Writes down whatever the group has to submit in writing.
  o **Time Keeper:** Informs the group when half the time is over and when there is one minute remaining.
  o **Reporter:** Gives an oral presentation to the class regarding the results of the group's work.
  o **Materials Manager:** Collects any resources or materials that the group needs to complete the task.
  o **Process Observer:** Gives the group feedback on how well they practiced their social skills during the assigned activity.

**WHO:**      Early and Middle Grades, High School

**WHEN:**      During a lesson

**THEME(S):**      All

- During cooperative learning activities, the concept of *individual accountability* helps to ensure that one person does not do all the work while every other person lets him or her. There are several ways to incorporate individual accountability. One way is to have all members initial the group's final product acknowledging that they agree with the answer and, if asked, could defend that answer to the class. Another way is to tell the class that at the culmination of the activity, you will select one person in the group to give the answer or make the presentation. Since group members do not know who that will be, every person needs to be prepared. Another way is to assign group roles so that each member is accountable at least for fulfilling the role to which they have been assigned. This was discussed in the previous activity.

**WHO:**        Early and Middle Grades, High School

**WHEN:**       During a lesson

**THEME(S):**   All

- One purpose of cooperative groups is to help students become more dependent on one another and less dependent on you. Oftentimes, students will bombard you with questions that other group members are able to answer. When this is happening, try this simple solution. Give each group three colored cards. Each time the group needs to ask you a question, they must give up one card. When all three cards are gone, you will not be able to answer any more questions for the group. Watch groups become more selective about the questions they choose to ask you.

**WHO:**        Early and Middle Grades, High School

**WHEN:**       During a lesson

**THEME(S):**   All

- When it is necessary for students to navigate through expository text, such as reading part of a social studies chapter, have them engage in *partner reading*. Have students work in pairs and take turns reading aloud to one another. They should read only loud enough for their partner to hear, or use their 6-inch voice. Students can decide whether they wish to read a page, read a paragraph, or pass their turn (*3-Ps*) until the selection is complete. English language learners may decide to pass their turn until they become more familiar with the language. Students could also take turns quizzing their partners regarding what was read.

**WHO:**        Early and Middle Grades, High School

**WHEN:**       During a lesson

**THEME(S):**   All

- Have students participate in the reading strategy *Save the Last Word for Me*. Have students read a portion of social studies text silently. Then have one student share something that was interesting to them in the text while others comment on what was shared. Finally, the original student closes out his or her share and passes the turn on to the next student.

**WHO:**        High School

**WHEN:**      During a lesson

**THEME(S):**    All

- Involve students in one form of a *Socratic Seminar* to help them become logical thinkers. Place students in small groups and then use the following seven steps to engage them in the process:

1. The teacher forms an *if . . . then assumption*. For example, *if democracy is good for America, then it is good for every other country in the world.*

2. Students discuss the assumption in their groups and then form a claim, or a proposition that they believe to be true. Each group writes their claim on a chart in a complete sentence and underlines key words. For example, *We believe that democracy is good for every country in the world.*

3. Students work together to come up with a working definition of the underlined key words and write the definition on the chart. *For example, the underlined key word is good. Exactly what does good mean?*

4. A spokesperson for each group cites evidence, by directly quoting from the source material, to support the group's claim.

5. Other groups might file a counterclaim, or find a flaw in the original group's thinking. The teacher also asks questions to help identify flaws.

6. The spokesperson from each group shares the group's main points, or summary of why they feel their claim is valid.

7. The last step is for students in each group to reexamine their claim in light of the discussion to see if they wish to change it, modify it, or retain it. The group then writes a paragraph or essay containing evidence that supports their conclusion (Delandtsheer, 2011).

## REFLECTION AND APPLICATION

How will I incorporate *reciprocal teaching and cooperative learning* into instruction to engage students' brains?

**Which reciprocal teaching and cooperative learning activities am I already incorporating into my social studies curriculum?**

**What additional activities will I incorporate?**

# Strategy 14

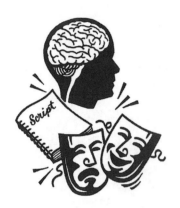

# Role Plays, Drama, Pantomimes, and Charades

## WHAT: DEFINING THE STRATEGY

Role play is one of the best strategies that social studies teachers have to put students in historical environments that they would not otherwise experience. It is one of my favorites to use when I teach a social studies lesson. For example, I was requested to teach a lesson on the four causes of World War II. I could have easily prepared and delivered a lecture on those causes. How boring! Instead, I placed the students into four cooperative groups, or families. Each family selected a facilitator and a scribe. I wrote each cause of World War II on separate index cards and had the facilitator from each group select a card. The job of each family was to use the information available to them (from their textbooks and/or the Internet) to research their selected cause and design a role play, involving all family members, which would inform the remainder of the class of their cause. The students worked extremely hard, but the lesson was also so much fun! In preparation for the role plays, students were practicing their parts so that they would appear believable when they performed their skits for the remainder of the class. At the end of the period, following the role plays, every student in that class could articulate the causes of World War II.

When students have the opportunity to experience what it must have been like to live or work during a particular period of history using role play, drama, simulations, or pantomimes or to act out their social studies vocabulary while playing charades, the information is more easily remembered since the concepts are more closely linked to real life. Whether you are teaching the concepts of migration or immigration, democracy or dictatorships, or imports or exports, have students design a role play and watch the magic and the memory!

112

# WHY: THEORETICAL FRAMEWORK

One way that historians learn about the past is through careful reconstruction of it (Melber & Hunter, 2010).

Simulations or role plays imitate real-world situations (Gregory & Herndon, 2010).

Role plays can assist students, particularly English language learners, in making abstract concepts more concrete (Sousa, 2011).

Role plays, or non-linguistic representations, give students a vehicle and contextual situation that helps them make sense out of new information (Gregory & Herndon, 2010).

Role plays can work best when students are illustrating important events, showing the process of a sequence, or demonstrating the role of a critical historical figure (Udvari-Solner & Kluth, 2008).

By giving students the option to express themselves through dramatic presentation, we launch them on a path to discovering their personal talents and preferences (Allen, 2008a).

*All the world's a stage—especially the classroom* (Allen, 2008a, p. 131).

Role plays can help students become aware of their individual beliefs and values (Sunal & Haas, 2005).

Students must understand the everyday lives of people who lived through historical events, and doing so through physical reenactment can result in fantastic learning gains (Putman & Rommel-Esham, 2004).

Drama is not only critical to effective instruction; teachers who use it give students the ability to learn and remember a lesson with ease and to discover how they feel about this strategy for expressing themselves (Allen, 2008a).

By performing role plays and, therefore, imagining other people's lives, students can be helped to envision multiple perspectives (Duncombe & Heikkinen, 1990).

# HOW: INSTRUCTIONAL ACTIVITIES

**WHO:**      Early and Middle Grades, High School

**WHEN:**     During a lesson

**THEME(S):**   All

Follow the steps below when engaging the class in a role play or simulation:

1. Present the topic or concept to students and give a brief overview of what a role play or simulation is;

2. Give students the procedures, rules, roles, scoring, and goals for the simulation;

3. Have students work through the role play while you monitor, facilitate and provide feedback; and

4. Debrief the activity and guide students in a discussion on how to apply what was learned during the simulation.

(Gregory & Herndon, 2010)

**WHO:**         Early and Middle Grades, High School

**WHEN:**        During a lesson

**THEME(S):**    Culture

- Have students plan and conduct a role play showing how conflict can be caused when two or more groups differ in their outlook regarding a particular issue. Place students in cooperative groups; then have each group select two or more conflicting groups of people and determine the source of the conflict. Then give the groups an allotted time period, such as 15 minutes, to plan a role play that depicts the problem. Have each group share their role play with the whole class.

**WHO:**         Middle Grades, High School

**WHEN:**        During a lesson

**THEME(S):**    Production, Distribution, and Consumption

- Have students develop and participate in a simulated economic system for the classroom where they design their own classroom currency and develop a system for using the currency to buy and sell goods and services for the classroom.

**WHO:**         Early and Middle Grades, High School

**WHEN:**        During a lesson

**THEME(S):**    Time, Continuity, and Change

- Have students design a role play that would demonstrate their knowledge of a past historical event such as the signing of the Declaration of Independence or the Great Depression.

**WHO:**         Middle Grades, High School

**WHEN:**        During a lesson

**THEME(S):**    Production, Distribution, and Consumption

- Turn your classroom into an assembly line to simulate what it must have been like to work in factories during the Industrial Revolution. Involve all students in producing a class product, where each individual student or pair of students does only one job repeatedly, which contributes to the overall production of the product. This simulation could be followed by a discussion of the advantages and disadvantages to the worker and production of an assembly line model.

**WHO:**          Middle Grades, High School

**WHEN:**        After a lesson

**THEME(S):**   Power, Authority, and Governance

- Have students work in cooperative groups of four to six to put an infamous historical figure on trial, such as Adolf Hitler or Stalin. Designate one student in each group as the prosecuting attorney and one as the defense attorney. Divide remaining group members in half and have them prepare either a defense or a prosecution for the group's client. Group members can be called as witnesses for either side and must be prepared with their testimony. Some class members who are not involved in the particular case can be appointed as jury members while you, the teacher, can serve as the judge. A choir robe works very well for your judicial garb and a gavel is easily accessible. You can also appoint a different bailiff for each trial. Not only will students learn facts of historical significance regarding an individual who changed history; they will simultaneously experience the inner workings of the judicial system.

**WHO:**          Middle Grades, High School

**WHEN:**        During a lesson

**THEME(S):**   People, Places, and Environment

- Have the class brainstorm names of women who played a significant role in history. For world history, such women could be Cleopatra, Joan of Arc, or Queen Elizabeth. For U.S. history, examples could be Abigail Adams, Harriett Tubman, Eleanor Roosevelt, or Rosa Parks. Place students in cooperative groups of four to six. Give each group a woman to research, including what the woman is known for, important events in the woman's life, three challenges faced and how she solved them, and three people who were important in the woman's life. Then have each group write a *Reader's Theater* script showing significant events in the woman's life, scenes showing the woman performing actions she is famous for, and the woman interacting with the three important people in her life. This role play should conclude with how people are better off today because of this woman's actions. Each *Reader's Theater* is then performed for the entire class.

**WHO:**          Early and Middle Grades, High School

**WHEN:**        During a lesson

**THEME(S):**   Power, Authority, and Governance

- During a local, state, or national election, have students examine the platform that each candidate proposes. Have them assume the place of one of the candidates, and write and deliver an issues speech. During the speech, students should attempt to anticipate the positions of the opposing candidate(s) so that they can be countered. Allow the class to hold a mock election in class or sponsor a school-wide election, and compare the results of these elections to those of the actual one.

**WHO:**         Early and Middle Grades, High School

**WHEN:**        During a lesson

**THEME(S):**    All

- Have students select a historical figure and plan a role play that depicts that person. Students will then take turns coming to the front of the class and acting as if they are that person. Class members should attempt to guess whom the student is emulating. To be convincing, each student should simulate some of the gestures and mannerisms of the person and should have prepared a short speech delivered in the first person. For example, *I am . . . I am known for . . . Here are a few of my accomplishments . . .*

**WHO:**         Middle Grades, High School

**WHEN:**        During a lesson

**THEME(S):**    Power, Authority, and Governance; Civic Ideals and Practices

- Create five or six real-life scenarios of situations where a person's first amendment or civil rights have or have not been violated. Put the scenarios on index cards. Put students in cooperative groups. Have each group select one card and design a role play, which would act out the situation. Have the class decide which right is being addressed and if the person's rights have or have not been violated.

**WHO:**         Middle Grades, High School

**WHEN:**        During a lesson

**THEME(S):**    Power, Authority, and Governance

- After reading the 1790 Petition from the Pennsylvania Abolition Society that urged Congress to promote the abolition of slavery, assign students a state and have them act as that state's senator. Have them create a list of arguments for or against abolition from the perspective of that state. Direct them to look at the social, political, economic, and cultural aspects of slavery. Then engage students in a debate regarding the issue.

**WHO:**        High School

**WHEN:**       During a lesson

**THEME(S):**   Civic Ideals and Practices

- Put students in cooperative groups of four to six. Give each group a controversial topic or issue in social studies. Examples could include advocating for Columbus, Vasco da Gama, Native Americans, or the Vikings. Other examples could include westward expansion, World War I, the Vietnam War, balancing the federal budget, fair tax, and so forth. Have students work together to research the pros and cons of the topic. Have one student take on the role of a lobbyist who argues for or against a particular position on the controversial topic while the group prepares the lobbyist to present the argument. Groups then take turns role playing by having the *lobbyist* persuade a panel of judges, legislators, or members of Congress to adopt their point of view. Students in the group can participate in the presentation while other members of the class serve as the audience in a town hall meeting, union hall, political club, or congressional caucus.

# REFLECTION AND APPLICATION

How will I incorporate *role plays, drama, pantomimes, and charades* into instruction to engage students' brains?

*Which role plays, drama, pantomimes, and charades am I already incorporating into my social studies curriculum?*

*What additional activities will I incorporate?*

# Strategy 15

# Storytelling

## WHAT: DEFINING THE STRATEGY

Allow me to tell you the following story:

> *There once was a man named **North**. His last name was **America**. He fell in love with a beautiful woman named **South**. They got married and she took his name so she became **South America**. They honeymooned in **Europe**. They were blessed to have four daughters. They named them all names beginning with the letter **A**. Their names were **Africa, Antarctica, Asia,** and **Australia*** (Tate, 2010).

What is history if it is not a story! In fact, the word *story* is in the word *history*. If you asked students to take an isolated list of the continents home and memorize them, many students would come back the next day without having done so. However, if you tell the aforementioned story to students not once, but several times, and then have them get up and retell the story to several students in class, students would more easily remember the continents.

I do not condone telling stories to students to waste their time. Any story you tell should be related to the social studies concept that you are teaching. In fact, if my history teachers had been great storytellers, I would still know the stories of history, even as an adult. Stories are connected together with a beginning, a middle, and an end, and the brain has an easy time of following a story. Try telling stories to your students or having your students create their own stories and watch their retention of content increase. When they remember your stories, they will remember your content. After all, isn't that the goal?

## WHY: THEORETICAL FRAMEWORK

When important historical events are tied to personal stories, the content becomes more relevant and, therefore, easier to remember (Melber & Hunter, 2010).

A good story holds the attention of and arouses the emotions of the storyteller as well as the listeners (Sylwester, 2010).

Comprehension in subject matter content is increased for middle- and upper-grade students with learning disabilities when those students are retelling the information from a reading passage, lecture, or story (Bender, 2008).

Processes that have specific steps, lists of things, and formulas can all be recalled easily using storytelling as a memory aid (Allen, 2008a).

For students with learning disabilities, storytelling involves the multiple language abilities of understanding the components of a story: using physical gestures, voice tone, and facial cues as well as understanding the cues from an audience (Bender, 2008).

Stories supply a script for us to tie information into our memories (Markowitz & Jensen, 2007).

Building as much visual imagery as possible into a story can make the story even more memorable for students (Allen, 2008a).

Storytelling can serve multiple purposes such as providing a memory device for students and increasing additional critical skills, such as literacy (Brand, 2006).

Asking students to form small groups and create their own stories helps them take ownership of those stories and, therefore, makes the information on which the stories are based more memorable (Allen, 2008a).

Ancient cultures have long practiced the tradition of storytelling in order to pass *memory* from one generation to the next (Markowitz & Jensen, 2007).

Having students from diverse backgrounds tell stories provides opportunities in the classroom to explore cultural diversity (Craig, Hull, Haggart, & Crowder, 2001).

## HOW: INSTRUCTIONAL ACTIVITIES

**WHO:**        Elementary and Middle Grades, High School

**WHEN:**       Before a lesson

**THEME(S):**   Individual Development and Identity

- Your students want to know your story! At the beginning of the term, give your social studies students opportunities to learn about you—your family, likes, dislikes, short- and long-term goals, and so forth. Students are naturally curious about their teacher, and this activity alone will go a long way toward helping you develop a relationship with your students. When I teach adults, at the beginning of my workshop, I give participants the opportunity to ask me any questions they want to in an effort to get to know me better. It gets the workshop off to a very positive start! The same thing will happen in your class.

**WHO:**          Elementary and Middle Grades, High School

**WHEN:**         Before a lesson

**THEME(S):**     All

- Create stories that are fictional or fact-based to illustrate a social studies concept that you are teaching. Make these stories a part of your lesson delivery and watch as you gain students' undivided attention and help them remember key concepts. If your story is funny or emotional, it will have even more of an impact on the brains of your students.

**WHO:**          Elementary and Middle Grades, High School

**WHEN:**         During or after a lesson

**THEME(S):**     Individual Development and Identity

- After you share your story, have students tell their stories! Have them write their personal autobiographies, which should include facts about their family, meaningful experiences while growing up, likes, dislikes, goals, and dreams. Students can volunteer to share their autobiographies with the class, which can lead to a discussion on how people know who they are and how people change over the years.

**WHO:**          Early and Middle Grades, High School

**WHEN:**         During a lesson

**THEME(S):**     Power, Authority, and Governance

- To remember the original 13 colonies, tell students the following story several times. This story was told to me by Gloria Caracas, El Oro Way Elementary School, Granada Hills, CA. Have students retell the story to at least three classmates. By the time they have heard the story several times and retold it several times, they will know the 13 colonies.

*There once was a cow named <u>Georgette</u> (**Georgia**). She was a <u>Jersey</u> (**New Jersey**) cow and gave lots of milk. She was strange because she liked to wear yellow <u>underwear</u> (**Delaware**). One day she went up the <u>Empire</u>*

*State Building* **(New York)**. *Up there she sang two Christmas* <u>Carols</u> **(North Carolina, South Carolina)**. *Then she came down and walked down the* <u>road</u> **(Rhode Island)**. *She was carrying a* <u>massive</u> **(Massachusetts)** <u>Virginia</u> **(Virginia)** <u>ham</u> **(New Hampshire)**. *She bent down to pick up a* <u>pencil</u> **(Pennsylvania)** *and proceeded to do a* <u>connect-a-dot</u> **(Connecticut)** *of* <u>Marilyn</u> **(Maryland)** *Monroe.*

**WHO:**          Elementary and Middle Grades, High School

**WHEN:**          During or after a lesson

**THEME(S):**     All

- Have students create original stories that are fictional or fact-based to help them remember a social studies concept that they need to recall. Stories are wonderful for helping students recall events that happen in sequential order. Have them retell their stories to several of their classmates. They can then remember their original stories every time they are asked to recall the concept on which the story is based.

**WHO:**          Middle Grades, High School

**WHEN:**          During a lesson

**THEME(S):**     All

- Place students in cooperative groups of four to six students. Give each group a major event that happened in the past, such as *The Holocaust* or *The Sinking of the Titanic*. Have each group research the event or situation and compare and contrast different stories or accounts of that event. Have them formulate possible reasons for the differences in the accounts.

**WHO:**          Early and Middle Grades, High School

**WHEN:**          During a lesson

**THEME(S):**     All

- When it would be beneficial to a concept you are teaching to have students read part of a social studies chapter in the textbook, divide the part into sections or chunks. Prior to having students read a chunk, give them a purpose for reading it, such as, *We are reading this next section to identify the role of a citizen in a democratic form of government as compared with a dictatorship.* Then provide time for students to read the section silently. Have them summarize the information in the section and retell it to a partner while answering the designated question.

**WHO:**          Elementary and Middle Grades, High School

**WHEN:**          Before a lesson

**THEME(S):**     Culture; Individual Development and Identity

- Capitalize on the diversity in your classroom by having students who were born outside of the United States volunteer to tell their individual stories of what it was like growing up in the culture of their birth. Only students who volunteer should be selected since some students of other cultures might be hesitant to tell their personal stories to the class. Have students compare and contrast various cultures by using the graphic organizer, called a *Venn Diagram*, contained in Chapter 5.

**WHO:**          Early or Middle Grades, High School

**WHEN:**          Before, during, or after a lesson

**THEME(S):**          All

- Have students select a book from your preapproved list of historical fiction or nonfiction books. Some sample lists follow. Have students brainstorm in cooperative groups a list of questions they would like to answer about their books. Have each group prioritize their lists and share them with the entire class. Have the entire class decide which questions will actually be used. Be sure that each group has one question from their list reflected in the final list. Have students read their book selection and complete in writing the list of student-generated questions. Students can participate in a jigsaw activity to share with other students about their books.

**WHO:**          Early and Middle Grades, High School

**WHEN:**          During a lesson

**THEME(S):**          All

- Incorporate children's books and other literary selections that have historical significance into instruction. These books not only address relevant historical characters and events; some even reinforce literary skills such as sequence of events or point of view. Some possible selections are listed below.

# MIDDLE AND HIGH SCHOOL NONFICTION BOOKS

*African-American Voices* by Deborah Gillan Straub (oral history of African American contributions to history)

*Art Up Close* by Claire d'Harcourt (artwork from various cultures, time periods, and mediums)

*Children Just Like Me: Celebrations* by Anabel Kindersley and Barbara Kindersley (visually celebrates the cultural traditions of children from around the world)

*A City Through Time* by Steve Noon (picture book depicting the growth of a city)

*The Diary of Anne Frank* by Anne Frank (the biography of a young girl living during the Holocaust)

*Encounter* by Jane Yolen (the story of Christopher Columbus from the Native's point of view)

*Funny Money* by Florence Temko (a fun book that teaches about U.S. money)

*Grandfather's Journey* by Allen Say (a book about the value of the immigrant experience)

*Hip Hop Around the World* by Lindsey Sanna (traces the history of hip hop from Jamaica and New York to Europe and Africa today)

*The Kid's Guide to Service Projects: Over 500 Service Ideas for Young People Who Want to Make a Difference* by Barbara Lewis (projects for young students who want to help others)

*The Lincoln-Douglas Debates* by Brendan January (description of seven debates between Lincoln and Douglas)

*My Brothers' Flying Machine* by Jane Yolen (the story of the Wright Brothers from the sister's point of view)

*The Silver Treasure: Myths and Legends of the World* by Geraldine McCaughrean (22 multicultural tales)

*Ultimate Field Trip 4: A Week in the 1800s* by Susan Goodman (helps prepare students for real and virtual field trips)

Consult the book *Integrating Language Arts and Social Studies: 25 Strategies for K–8 Inquiry-Based Learning* by Leah Melber and Alyce Hunter for a more extensive list of children's literature connections.

**WHO:**        Early and Middle Grades, High School

**WHEN:**       After a lesson

**THEME(S):**   All

- Assist or have your librarian assist students in locating historical fiction stories or nonfiction biographies, which can accompany a particular period of history you are teaching. By having students get involved in the real life of a main character, students can see history through their eyes, and it therefore becomes more relevant and meaningful. Below is an abbreviated list of historical novels appropriate for middle and high school students.

# ■ MIDDLE AND HIGH SCHOOL BOOKS BY SUBJECT

## Historical Novels

*The Bad Queen* by Carolyn Meyer (2010)—story of Marie-Antoinette, the extravagant and doomed last queen of France*

*Beowulf: Dragonslayer* by Rosemary Sutcliff (1961)—a retelling of the Anglo-Saxon story of the warrior who defeats a terrible monster who has been killing the king's men*

*The Book of the Lion* by Michael Cadnum (2000)—story of a 17-year-old boy who serves as a squire to a knight on his way to join Richard the Lionheart's army in the Holy Land during the Third Crusade*

*Fallen Grace* by Mary Hooper (2011)—story of an orphaned girl in 1861 London who has to look after her simpleminded sister and accepts work as a paid mourner at well-to-do funerals*

*Fever, 1793* by Laurie Halse Anderson (2000)—story of a 16-year-old girl in Philadelphia trying to find her mother during an epidemic of yellow fever

*The Fighting Ground* by Avi (1994)—story of a 13-year-old boy during the Revolutionary War*

*My Brother Sam Is Dead* by James Collier (1974)—tragedy strikes the Meeker family when the oldest son joins the rebel forces while the rest of the family tries to remain neutral during the American Revolution

*The Red Badge of Courage* by Stephen Crane (1895)—Henry Fleming's attitude toward war changes while he is a Union soldier

*Sacajawea* by Joseph Bruchac (2000)—story of the young Shoshone woman who bore a child and served as an interpreter and guide for the Lewis and Clark Expedition while still in her teens*

*Sarah, Plain and Tall* by Patricia MacLachlan (1985)—story of two farm children whose father marries a woman from Maine who answers his advertisement for a wife*

*Sarny* by Gary Paulsen (1993)—story of a young woman freed from slavery at the end of the Civil War who sets out to find her children, sold South just days before the war ended*

*The Scribes From Alexandria* by Caroline Lawrence (2008)—story of four friends separated when they are shipwrecked in a storm near the Egyptian city of Alexandria*

*An Unlikely Friendship* by Ann Rinaldi (2007)—story of Mary Todd Lincoln and her best friend, a black dressmaker*

*Walk the Dark Streets* by Edith Baer (1998)—story of a Jewish girl growing up in Germany from 1933 to 1940 as Hitler begins World War II

*Winter's Knight* by Richard Argent (2010)—historical fantasy about a teen who becomes a Crusader in order to fulfill the glorious fate he believes he has been promised

*Witch Child* by Celia Rees (2001)—novel written as a journal by a 14-year-old girl who immigrates from England to a Puritan community and confesses to being a witch*

*Indicates that the author has written a number of additional books in this same genre.

**WHO:**          Middle Grades, High School

**WHEN:**        Before, during, or after a lesson

**THEME(S):**   All

- Have your middle and high school students select notable trade books based on social studies topics and genres. Some recommended titles are as follows:

## Biography

*Anne Frank: Her Life in Words and Pictures.* Menno Metselaar and Ruud van der Rol. Translated by Arnold J. Pomerans. Roaring Brook Press/Flash Point, an Imprint of Macmillan Children's Publishing Group. 216 pp.

*Catherine the Great: Empress of Russia (A Wicked History™).* Zu Vincent. Illustrated by Mark Summers and Raphael Montoliu. Franklin Watts. 128 pp.

*Our Country's First Ladies.* Ann Bausum. Illustrated with prints and photographs. National Geographic Society. 128 pp.

*The Rise and Fall of Senator Joe McCarthy.* James Cross Giblin. Clarion/Houghton Mifflin Harcourt. 304 pp.

*Up Close: Rachel Carson.* Ellen Levine. Viking Children's Books, an imprint of Penguin Young Readers Group. 224 pp.

*Up Close: Ronald Reagan.* James Sutherland. Viking Children's Books. 256 pp.

## Contemporary Issues

*Camel Rider.* Prue Mason. Charlesbridge. 208 pp.
*Dear Author: Letters of Hope. Top Young Adult Authors Respond to Kids' Toughest Issues.* Edited by Joan F. Kaywell. Philomel Books, a division of Penguin Young Readers Group. 272 pp.

## Economics

*Lawn Boy.* Gary Paulsen. Wendy Lamb Books, an imprint of Random House Children's Books. 96 pp.
*Show Me the Money: How to Make Cents of Economics.* Alvin Hall. DK Publishing. 96 pp.

## Geography

*Battling in the Pacific: Soldiering in World War II (Soldiers on the Battlefront).* Susan Provost Beller. Twenty-First Century Books, a division of Lerner Publishing Group. 112 pp.
*Sunrise Over Fallujah.* Walter Dean Myers. Scholastic Press. 304 pp.

## History

*The Brothers' War: Civil War Voices in Verse.* J. Patrick Lewis. Illustrated with photographs. National Geographic Society. 48 pp.
*The Crimson Cap.* Ellen Howard. Holiday House. 208 pp.
*Cracker! The Best Dog in Vietnam.* Cynthia Kadohata. Atheneum Books for Young Readers. 320 pp.
*Diamonds in the Shadow.* Caroline B. Cooney. Delacorte Press, an imprint of Random House Children's Books. 240 pp.
*Fire From the Rock.* Sharon M. Draper. Dutton Children's Books, a division of Penguin Young Readers Group. 240 pp.
*First People: An Illustrated History of American Indians.* David C. King. DK Publishing. 192 pp.
*Gibson Girls and Suffragists: Perceptions of Women From 1900 to 1918 (Images and Issues of Women in the Twentieth Century).* Catherine Gourley. Twenty-First Century Books, a division of Lerner Publishing Group. 144 pp. Also recommended in this series: *Flappers and the New American Woman: Perceptions of Women From 1918 through the 1920s.* Catherine Gourley. Twenty-First Century Books, a division of Lerner Publishing Group. 144 pp.
*Hidden on the Mountain: Stories of Children Sheltered From the Nazis in Le Chambon.* Deborah Durland DeSaix & Karen Gray Ruelle. Holiday House. 275 pp.
*Home of the Brave.* Katherine Applegate. Feiwel and Friends, an imprint of Macmillan. 249 pp.
*On the Wings of Heroes.* Richard Peck. Dial Books for Young Readers, a division of Penguin Young Readers Group. 160 pp.
*The Real Benedict Arnold.* Jim Murphy. Illustrated with archival prints. Clarion Books. 272 pp.
*Revolution Is Not a Dinner Party.* Ying Chang Compestine. Henry Holt and Company. 256 pp.

*Three Cups of Tea: One Man's Journey to Change the World . . . One Child at a Time.* Greg Mortenson and David Oliver Relin. Dial Books for Young Readers, an imprint of Penguin Young Readers Group. 240 pp.

*A Tugging String: A Novel About Growing Up During the Civil Rights Era.* David T. Greenberg. Dutton Children's Books. 176 pp.

*Two Girls of Gettysburg.* Lisa Klein. Bloomsbury Children's Books. 400 pp.

*The Ultimate Weapon: The Race to Develop the Atom Bomb.* Edward T. Sullivan. Holiday House. 208 pp.

*Uprising.* Margaret Peterson Haddix. Simon & Schuster Books for Young Readers. 352 pp.

*Views From the Scopes Trial.* Jen Bryant. Alfred A. Knopf/Random House Children's Books. 240 pp.

*Without Warning: Ellen's Story 1914–1918.* Dennis Hamley. Candlewick Press. 336 pp.

# REFLECTION AND APPLICATION

How will I incorporate *storytelling* into instruction to engage students' brains?

**Which storytelling activities am I already incorporating into my social studies curriculum?**

**What additional activities will I incorporate?**

# Strategy 16

# Technology

## WHAT: DEFINING THE STRATEGY

It appears that when it comes to technology, our current culture is divided into two major groups—*Digital Natives* and *Digital Immigrants* (Prensky, 2009). I now realize that my three children fall into the category of digital natives since for the majority of their lives, they have easily mastered a variety of interactive technologies. I have seen my children multitask on a computer screen while simultaneously talking on their cell phones and responding verbally to an occasional question on my part. After all, they don't know anything else! Conversely, I am a digital immigrant and have slowly come to use the new technologies one step at a time, and not always easily, I must admit!

For example, when I wanted to convert to using an iPod rather than CDs for the music in my workshops, I had to turn to my 26-year-old daughter, Jessica, for training. She was the teacher and I became the student. It took more than three separate sessions, but eventually, Jessica taught me how to download music from my many CDs; how to buy music from the Internet; how to locate music on the iPod by artist, album, or song; and how to make playlists for the 10 different courses that I teach. If I am stuck on the computer, I can call my son, Chris, and he knows how to *unstick* me.

In the 21st century, thanks to modern technology, students have the capability of having access to large amounts of readily available information and data at the click of a computer. Today in the social studies classroom, this is a definite advantage. Years ago, students did not have this privilege. However, while technology is one of the eight basic competencies that students need in order to be successful in the workplace, its overuse can come with a price. When students fail to balance the strategy of technology with the other 19 brain-compatible strategies outlined in this book, certain other areas can suffer. I don't know if you have noticed or not, but as I interact with students during the model lessons I teach, I have been noticing that some students appear to be losing their social or interpersonal skills or to have never developed them in the first place. As I stand at the classroom door and greet students, I have noted that the numbers of students who cannot give me eye contact, shake my hand, and say *Good Morning!* seems to be increasing. However, the need for interpersonal or social skills and the ability to work with people from diverse backgrounds is also one of the eight competencies that students need to be successful following graduation. This can be better achieved through the strategy of cooperative learning. Even cyber-bullying is on the rise. It is so much easier to say disrespectful things to and about you if I don't have to do it face-to-face.

The use of technology is crucial for effective social studies instruction. But, don't forget, so are the other 19 strategies.

## WHY: THEORETICAL FRAMEWORK

Allowing English language learners to integrate technology enables them to extend their learning to higher levels of cognitive engagement (Sousa, 2011).

In order to practice thinking critically, students must have the ability to acquire information and conduct research by using a variety of technologies designed to analyze, synthesize, interpret, and evaluate information (National Council for the Social Studies, 2010).

If students exit schools without the basic technical skills of keyboarding, using databases and spreadsheets, reading technical manuals, and using fax machines, e-mailing, wireless technology, the Web, and online services, they will not be equipped to enter higher education or the world of work (Fogarty, 2009).

Students can develop more positive attitudes toward learning when they work cooperatively with other students and integrate technology while engaged in authentic complex tasks (Sousa, 2011).

When teachers assess students' skills in technology, they can engage students in projects that will allow them to learn new skills while also challenging them (Gregory & Herndon, 2010).

Some of the computer-based and media/communication technology skills required of students in the social studies classroom include the following:

the ability to operate input devices and other appropriate multimedia sources; the ability to use the Internet and online information; the ability to use tools for research, problem solving, and decision making; and the ability to utilize tools and resources to manage information (National Council for the Social Studies, 2010).

The Internet has created a huge amount of knowledge and information for students meaning that *the library doors expand the globe* and students' dendrites and synaptic connections are increased accordingly (Feinstein, 2009).

Technology can integrate each of Howard Gardner's multiple intelligences in many ways and, therefore, serves as an invaluable tool to accommodate students' various learning styles (Gregory & Herndon, 2010).

Technology can assist students of all ability levels to *process, demonstrate, retain, and share information and communication* (Karten, 2009, p. 196).

One study found that some computer games, which closely simulated real life, were more likely to increase attention, reduce hyperactivity, and improve memory and creativity in middle-school age students (Fernandez & Klingberg, 2006).

Digital-age literacy includes an understanding of economics and global issues and the ability to use the technology for analyzing information (Sheffield, 2007).

Technology is only the tool for delivering the lesson and not the lesson itself (Hiraoka, 2006).

# HOW: INSTRUCTIONAL ACTIVITIES

**WHO:**       Early Grades

**WHEN:**      During a lesson

**THEME(S):**  Power, Authority, and Governance

- Model for students how to use the *Kidspiration* program on the computer by having the class explain the structure of their elementary school on a graphic organizer. For example, the name of the school would be in the center bubble with the Principal, Assistant Principal, and Teachers' Names and Grade Levels or Jobs leading from the center. Have students practice drawing the arrows to another bubble. After all the information has been typed, show the students how to add graphics and color, change the font size, and so forth. Explain that this graphic organizer is just like the branches of the federal government that we will be discussing and drawing later.

**WHO:**        High School

**WHEN:**        During a lesson

**THEME(S):**        Production, Distribution, and Consumption

- Place students in cooperative groups of four to six students. Assign or have each group select a current global issue such as immigration, health care, or global warming. Have them research different perspectives and use technology to develop a media presentation, which shares their findings with the class (National Council for the Social Studies, 2010).

**WHO:**        Early and Middle Grades, High School

**WHEN:**        During a lesson

**THEME(S):**        Science, Technology, and Society

- Engage students in an age-appropriate project where they must research the advantages and negative consequences of the use of technology in the school (early grades), community (middle grades), and world-at-large (high school). Have them present this project using a type of technology of their choosing, such as a PowerPoint presentation, a videotaping of a role play, and so forth.

**WHO:**        Early and Middle Grades, High School

**WHEN:**        After a lesson

**THEME(S):**        Culture; Science, Technology, and Society

- Locate a class or classes living in another country that would be willing to serve as pen pals for your students. Pair each student with a corresponding student from the other country. Have them communicate with one another via e-mail. Set parameters for how often the communication should take place and what topics can and cannot be addressed. Through this activity, not only will students vicariously experience the life of a peer from another culture, but the following five steps of writing a friendly letter can also be addressed: heading, greeting, body, closing, and signature. The two largest Web sites for pen-paling are Penworld and EpalsConnect, which have more than half a million members each. Postcrossing is an international project that links people from around the world through the exchange of postcards.

**WHO:**        Middle Grades, High School

**WHEN:**        After a lesson

**THEME(S):**        All

- Have students develop a role play depicting a historical event, such as Washington crossing the Delaware or the signing of the Declaration of Independence. Once the role play has been practiced enough to be perfected, have students videotape the role play and post it to YouTube for other students to access throughout the world.

**WHO:**　　　　Middle Grades, High School

**WHEN:**　　　After a lesson

**THEME(S):**　Culture; Science, Technology, and Society

- Engage students in a whole class discussion on the following topic: *How have technological advances both improved and detracted from the quality of our lives?* Assist them in seeing that a balance of time and effort spent engaged in technological pursuits with that spent interacting face-to-face with family, friends, and peers may be preferable.

**WHO:**　　　　Middle Grades, High School

**WHEN:**　　　During a lesson

**THEME(S):**　Power, Authority, and Governance

- Divide students into groups of four to six. Have each group create a documentary about the causes, course, and consequences of the Holocaust, collapse of the Soviet Union, or reunification of Germany. The group's documentary may be in the form of a PowerPoint, poster, storyboard, Movie Maker, Photo Story, or photographic time line. Have each group share its documentary with the remainder of the class, explaining their understanding of the event and its impact on the modern world.

**WHO:**　　　　Early and Middle Grades, High School

**WHEN:**　　　Before, during, and after a lesson

**THEME(S):**　All

- Integrate videos clips or have students integrate videos clips into social studies instruction. Videos can be used to introduce a new topic or to summarize or close a lesson; to incorporate into a PowerPoint presentation; to provide a common experience for a class discussion; or to check for student understanding by questioning before, during, or following the video presentation (Gregory & Herndon, 2010).

**WHO:**　　　　Early and Middle Grades, High School

**WHEN:**　　　During a lesson

**THEME(S):**　All

- Introduce video streaming as a resource for your social studies presentations or your students' so that information is in its most current form. Two Web sites that provide video for downloading include PBS Video (http://video.pbs.org) and Discovery Education (www .discoveryeducation.com/index/cfm) (Gregory & Herndon, 2010).

| | |
|---|---|
| **WHO:** | Middle Grades, High School |
| **WHEN:** | During a lesson |
| **THEME(S):** | Power, Authority, and Governance |

- Have students work in pairs or small groups to create a Bill of Rights Glogster. Assign each pair or group a different amendment, and have them research the historical implications of the amendment. Tell them that their product must include the original reason for the amendment, appropriate court cases, video, and audio that represents each amendment without using actual words from the amendment in the product. Then, have students share their product while the remainder of the class attempts to guess the amendment depicted.

| | |
|---|---|
| **WHO:** | Middle Grades, High School |
| **WHEN:** | During a lesson |
| **THEME(S):** | Power, Authority, and Governance |

- Provide for students a large list of significant events that occurred during the Civil Rights movement. Allow them to pick any 10 events and create a time line for those events. Each date on the time line must be accompanied with a visual, the significance of the event, a connection to another date on the time line, and the specifics (who, what, when, where, why). This project can be turned in digitally, with all students completing their work in PowerPoint or by using a free online time line creation program, such as www.xtimeline .com. If completed digitally, projects from all students can be combined into a very detailed time line of Civil Rights events.

| | |
|---|---|
| **WHO:** | Early and Middle Grades, High School |
| **WHEN:** | Before, during, and after a lesson |
| **THEME(S):** | All |

- Below is a list of Web-based resources that can be integrated into your lessons as you deliver content in a variety of social studies areas.

# ■ WEB-BASED RESOURCES BY SUBJECT

## American and U.S. History

*Adventure Tales of America by Jody Potts* (free online illustrated texts)
http://www.adventuretales.com/index.html

*Interactive United States History Map*
http://www.learner.org/interactives/historymap/index.html

*Freedom: The History of US* (webisodes of the history of the U.S. from PBS)
http://www.pbs.org/wnet/historyofus/menu.html

*PBS for Teachers* (online lesson plans and instructional materials that correspond to Public Broadcasts)
http://www.pbs.org/teachers/

## Economics

*The Mint* (an interactive site on personal finance for middle and high school students)
http://www.themint.org/

*Consumer Action Website* (access to the federal government's Consumer Action Handbook and links to a consumer directory)
http://www.consumeraction.gov/

*CNN: Money.com* (current information and events in the world of economics)
http://money.cnn.com/news/economy/

*PBS: Your Life, Your Money* (interactive resources for personal financial literacy)
http://www.pbs.org/your-life-your-money/index.php

*Visualizing Economics* (maps, charts, and graphs on U.S. and world economics)
http://www.visualizingeconomics.com/

*Federal Reserve* (helps students understand the workings of the Federal Reserve Bank)
http://www.federalreserve.org

## Government

*American Bar Association* (interactive lessons, conversation starters, lesson plans, and more for the study of the U.S. Constitution)
http://abaconstitution.org

*Street Law: Landmark Cases of the Supreme Court* (a full range of resources and activities to support the teaching of landmark Supreme Court cases)
http://www.streetlaw.org/en/landmark.aspx

*iCivics* (a project that uses gaming and simulations to teach students civics and inspire them to be active participants in a democratic society; designed for middle school students by Justice Sandra Day O'Connor)
http://www.icivics.org/

*The U.S. House of Representatives*
http://kids.clerk.house.gov/

*The U.S. Senate*
http://www.senate.gov/

*The Supreme Court of the United States*
http://www.supremecourt.gov/

(The websites listed above help students understand the workings of the branches of the federal government.)

## World Geography

*World Mapper* (more than 700 maps and cartograms of the world)
http://www.worldmapper.org/

*United Nations: Cyber Schoolbus* (online games, lesson plans, and information on current events, and data from countries around the world)
http://www.un.org/Pubs/CyberSchoolBus/index.shtml

*Tag Galaxy* (provides copyright free visuals or pictures that illustrate concepts)
http://www.taggalaxy.com/

*The Next Vista: Global Views* (a collection of video introductions to different cultures around the world produced by teenagers)
http://www.nextvista.org/collection-list-global-views/

*Gapminder* (interactive statistical information on world trends)
http://www.gapminder.org/

## World History

*World History for Us All* (a clearinghouse of lesson plans and resources developed by world history teachers and sponsored by San Diego State University)
http://worldhistoryforusall.sdsu.edu/

*Federal Resources for Educational Excellence* (rich library of lesson plans and resources from the federal government)
http://free.ed.gov/subjects.cfm?subject _id=22&toplvl=12

*Center for History and News Media* (provides access to abundant documents, paintings, photographs, and art and how to use them in the classroom
http://chnm.gmu.edu/worldhistorysources/index.html

*PBS Teachers* (provides a PBS lesson bank and programs for rich World History resources)
http://www.pbs.org/teachers/socialstudies

*Exploring Ancient World Cultures* (Web resources for the ancient world)
http://eawc.evansville.edu/index.htm

## Generic Social Studies Web Sites

http://www.socialstudiesforkids.com
http://www.smithsonianeducation.org
http://www.historyplace.com
http://www.teachinghistory.org
http://www.kids.gov
http://www.free.ed.gov

## REFLECTION AND APPLICATION

> How will I incorporate *technology* into
> instruction to engage students' brains?

*Which technological activities am I already incorporating into my social studies curriculum?*

*What additional activities will I incorporate?*

# Strategy 17

# Visualization and Guided Imagery

## WHAT: DEFINING THE STRATEGY

Visuals are things you can see with your eyes. Visualization is seeing with the mind and it is so effective that people use it in the real world all of the time. Athletes are taught to visualize themselves scoring the touchdown or hitting the homerun before the game begins to increase the likelihood that those things will occur during the game. David Sousa, author of *How the Brain Learns* (2006) and many other books on the brain, relates that when visualizing, the same parts of the brain's visual cortex are activated as when the eyes are actually receiving and processing information from the real world. That is how powerful visualization can be!

I am told that the pilots from the beautiful Blue Angels fighter squadron, which executes those incredible maneuvers in the sky, actually sit together in a room prior to getting in their planes to practice their routine. The pilot in the lead plane calls out the maneuvers that they are expected to demonstrate. All the other pilots visualize what is being called. Then, only when the routine is completed in their minds do they go to their planes and actually practice the routine in the air.

Why not have your social studies students visualizing concepts that you want them to remember? For example, when teaching about the Civil War, you could first show some visuals depicting the action in one or more famous battles. Then, following that, you could have students use every one of their senses to see in their minds what it must have been like to be on that battlefield. Use guided imagery to have them imagine what the soldiers would have seen, what they would have heard, what they would have smelled, what tastes would be in their mouths, what they would have felt with their hands, and what feelings would be in their hearts as they fought. You could even vividly describe the scene orally as students are visualizing it in their minds. This technique would go a long way toward creating empathy for what others may have experienced in history and also ensuring that students remember a particular time period since they cannot experience the period firsthand.

## WHY: THEORETICAL FRAMEWORK

When the names and dates of important events in history are too abstract to remember, visual imagery makes those events easier to retain (Melber & Hunter, 2010).

Imagery can provide the brain with more mind/body control and has also been shown to change the chemistry of the body (Markowitz & Jensen, 2007).

A story is made more memorable for students if the teacher builds into the story as much visual imagery as possible (Allen, 2008a).

*A picture in your mind creates a memory you can find* (Sprenger, 2007, p. 33).

The basis for many mnemonic tools is the brain's ability to visualize abstract information into images that are concrete (Markowitz & Jensen, 2007).

Generating mental pictures or visualizing is one activity that aids students in the nonlinguistic (or mental) processing of information (Marzano, 2007).

To recall a list of items, those items should be connected together in the imagination or visualized crashing together; underneath or beside one another; or dancing or playing together (Markowitz & Jensen, 2007).

Visualizing a scene can be part of a mental warm-up early in class for unmotivated learners. Other parts of the warm-up include physical stretching, role playing, creating questions, brainstorming, or problem solving (Jensen, 2008).

During a study at Oxford University, a group of elementary school children who practiced visualizing prior to taking a test scored higher on the test than did the control group who simply took the test (Drake, 1996).

Since the image is the greatest instrument of instruction, most of class time should be spent ensuring that students are forming proper images. This would make teaching much easier (Dewey, 1938).

# HOW: INSTRUCTIONAL ACTIVITIES

**WHO:**  Early and Middle Grades, High School

**WHEN:**  Before a lesson

**THEME(S):**  All

- A sizable percentage of a person's success in any endeavor has to do with their confidence or belief that they can be successful. Giving a failing student one more grade of *F* does not bolster that confidence. After all, we know from watching sports that *success breeds success!* One baseball player who gets a hit will often get another hit later in the game since the first hit gave his or her brain confidence. Have students visualize themselves being successful in your social studies class. Have them picture themselves volunteering answers, turning in homework, scoring high on tests, and earning a great grade at the culmination of a quarter, semester, or year. By incorporating the brain-compatible strategies with students, you will build on one success to the next so that even students who have not done well in the past gain confidence in your classroom.

**WHO:**  Early and Middle Grades, High School

**WHEN:**  During a lesson

**THEME(S):**  All

- As you or your students read a social studies text, have them engage every one of their senses (sight, hearing, taste, touch, and smell) visualizing the scenes depicted in the text. When the brain visualizes, it goes through a process similar to what it would go through if the student had actually been there.

**WHO:**  Early and Middle Grades, High School

**WHEN:**  During a lesson

**THEME(S):**  All

- As you tell your students a story that would help them remember a particular social studies concept, have them engage every one of their senses (sight, hearing, taste, touch, and smell) visualizing the scenes depicted in the story you are telling. The more emotional or weird you can make the story, the more memorable the visualization. I was in the social studies classroom of a middle school teacher when he was telling the story of what happened to the body when someone contracted the Bubonic Plague. His story was so gross and disgusting that no middle school student in that class would ever forget it!

**WHO:**  Early and Middle Grades, High School

**WHEN:**  After a lesson

**THEME(S):**  All

- Have students work independently or in groups to create a visual image that would link a social studies concept to its definition. The more absurd the visual image, the easier it is for the brain to remember. For example, to recall the concept of a *dictatorship,* have students visualize a man with a mean look on his face *dictating* a letter to his secretary. The letter would tell the secretary what she could or could not do and what would happen if she disobeyed his orders!

**WHO:**  Early and Middle Grades, High School

**WHEN:**  During a lesson

**THEME(S):**  All

- Have students mentally transport themselves to a specific period of history currently being studied, such as the French Revolution or the Harlem Renaissance. Have them imagine how they would be dressed, with whom they would talk, what their profession would be, where they would live, how long they would live, and so forth.

**WHO:**  Early and Middle Grades, High School

**WHEN:**  During a lesson

**THEME(S):**  People, Places, and Environments

- Have students visualize an apple sitting on a pole in the middle of land to help them remember that the capital of Maryland is Annapolis.

**WHO:**  Early and Middle Grades, High School

**WHEN:**  During a lesson

**THEME(S):**  People, Places, and Environments

- Have students visualize a saint sipping on a little bitty soda to help them remember that the capital of Minnesota is St. Paul.

**WHO:**  Early and Middle Grades, High School

**WHEN:**  During a lesson

**THEME(S):**  All

- When students have to remember social studies vocabulary words or concepts, have them create their own original visualizations that link the concept to be remembered to its definition. When students create these visual images themselves, they stand a better chance of remembering them when the time comes.

**WHO:**    Early and Middle Grades, High School

**WHEN:**    During a lesson

**THEME(S):**    All

- When students have to link social studies concepts, events, or objects in a particular sequence, have them visualize the items in the sequence somehow connected together. Have them imagine those items being tossed about, crashing into one another, upside down, backwards, dancing together, or positioned in a number of unique ways. These images will help to ensure that the sequence is remembered since the brain likes novelty, and these items will be visualized in novel ways.

**WHO:**    Early and Middle Grades, High School

**WHEN:**    During a lesson

**THEME(S):**    All

- *RIDER* is a visual imagery strategy that helps students with learning disabilities comprehend what is read. *RIDER* is an acronym for *Read* the sentence, *Imagine* a picture in the mind, *Describe* how the new and old image differ, *Evaluate* to determine if the image shows everything, and *Repeat* as the next sentence is read (Bender, 2008). This technique is not only effective for students with learning disabilities; it is effective with all students.

## REFLECTION AND APPLICATION

> How will I incorporate *visualization and guided imagery* into instruction to engage students' brains?

*Which visualization and guided imagery activities am I already incorporating into my social studies curriculum?*

*What additional activities will I incorporate?*

# Strategy 18

# Visuals

## WHAT: DEFINING THE STRATEGY

I will never forget a lesson that I taught to some kindergarten students several years ago. If you want to feel good and forget your troubles, just visit a prekindergarten or kindergarten classroom. Some of the things they say are hilarious! On this particular day, the lesson involved distinguishing whether to use a map or a globe depending on what information we wanted to find. Since I knew we needed visuals, I brought to class a map and a globe and placed them in front of the students. We then had a discussion of what we could find out from each visual. Following the discussion, during which every student wanted to add a personal comment, some of which had nothing to do with the lesson, I gave the kindergartners an oral quiz. I provided them with a real-life situation and they had to tell me whether it would be better to use a map or a globe to locate information that would help us in the situation. My first question was, *Which one would you use if you wanted to find the name of a street in your neighborhood—a map or a globe?* To which one student promptly replied, *I know all the streets in my neighborhood, so I don't need either one.* Moving right along! The second question was, *Suppose I wanted to know which is the best way to go if I were flying in an airplane to another country.* To which one student promptly responded, *My mother is afraid to fly and so am I, so I don't want to go to another country.* You can see that I was not gaining much ground!

The lesson continued and soon I was able to determine that most students knew when to use a map and when to use a globe, plus I had spent a wonderful morning laughing at the unexpected answers from a delightful group of students. Having the visuals of an actual map and a globe so that students could see for themselves was so beneficial to my lesson. When they say, *A picture is worth a thousand words,* they are truly serious. The brain remembers what it sees. Learn how to incorporate this strategy into your social studies lessons and watch student retention and understanding improve!

# WHY: THEORETICAL FRAMEWORK

Visuals help students retain content longer since the eyes contain approximately *70% of the body's sensory receptors and send millions of signals every second along optic nerves to the visual processing centers of the brain* (Patricia Wolfe in Hyerle & Alper, 2011, p. xiii).

As a teacher lectures, particularly to struggling English language learners, key concepts and vocabulary from the lecture should be written on the board or a flip chart as a visual and used to fill in accompanying graphic organizers or listening guides during the lecture (Sousa, 2011).

Every visual should in some way relate to the content so that when students' attention strays from the lesson, there will be something visual from which they can learn (including classroom maps, student projects, and so forth) (Delandtsheer, 2011).

Identifying visual features of the text such as charts, graphs, maps, illustrations, and headings is a research-based literacy strategy that should be used prior to reading (National Council for the Social Studies, 2010).

Students, especially those who are visual learners, like to look at the paintings of history to ascertain what the artist chose to depict and to consider the total design and artistic elements that make up the composition (Melber & Hunter, 2010).

Instructional strategies that pair visual stimuli with auditory stimuli will support learners who have problems with auditory processing (Green & Casale-Giannola, 2011).

The use of a picture, or a visual, can serve to aid the memory of all students, including those with learning disabilities, since memories appear to last much longer when they are associated with pictures (Bender, 2008).

Visuals assist students who have trouble focusing on the lesson since they provide them with a focal point on which to place their attention (Algozzine, Campbell, & Wang, 2009a).

Personal photos are visuals that can be very effective in helping students (especially English language learners and students with disabilities) make the connection between social studies standards and personal family history (Tanner, 2008).

Visual aids provide students with a focal point and improve their learning as they move through the following stages of acquiring new concepts: acquisition, proficiency, maintenance, and generalization (Algozzine, Campbell, & Wang, 2009b).

Props, peripherals, and positive affirming posters can be used to reinforce the learning for students and increase the visual impact of the classroom (Perez, 2008).

# HOW: INSTRUCTIONAL ACTIVITIES

**WHO:**        Early and Middle Grades, High School

**WHEN:**       Before, during, and after a lesson

**THEME(S):**   All

- Whether you know it or not, your students are watching you as you are providing direct instruction. You are the best visual for getting across your social studies content to your students. Don't be a boring lecturer. Use gestures, hand movements, and voice inflections to display your enthusiasm about the content you are teaching. If you are not excited about social studies, don't expect students to be! Change your location in the classroom. That will help you gain and keep their attention. Remember to *teach on your feet, not in a seat!*

**WHO:**        Early and Middle Grades, High School

**WHEN:**       Before, during, and after a lesson

**THEME(S):**   All

- Use the walls of your social studies classroom as a visual support system for your students. Have local, state, and world maps easily accessible so that as content is taught, students can easily get up and find a particular location being discussed. Pertinent graphic organizers, word webs, and word walls also could be displayed, which could serve as constant reminders of the social studies vocabulary previously taught. When your students are not watching you, they will still visually take in the peripherals around the room. That action alone enhances learning.

**WHO:**        Early and Middle Grades, High School

**WHEN:**       During a lesson

**THEME(S):**   Time, Continuity, and Change

- As you study specific events in history or historical periods, construct or have students construct a time line on the wall as a visual. As the school year progresses, add events studied to the time line. Not only will this serve as a visual reminder of the relationships of sequential events in history, but if the time line is ever removed, students can still visualize it as if it were still on the wall.

**WHO:**        Early Grades

**WHEN:**       During a lesson

**THEME(S):**   All

- Bring to class an example of a map, a globe, an almanac, an atlas, and other reference sources. Put students in cooperative groups of four to six students. Give each group a different reference and have them determine what social studies questions could be answered using the source to which they have been assigned. Then have each group report to the entire class what they have decided.

**WHO:**          Early and Middle Grades, High School

**WHEN:**        During a lesson

**THEME(S):**   All

- Before your students read their social studies textbook, have them survey the chapter or unit of study to ascertain what the chapter will address. Have them peruse visuals such as bold headings, subheadings, maps, charts, graphs, pictures, and captions. Have them make predictions as to what the chapter will include. This technique goes by the mnemonic device *SQ3R* (**Survey** the chapter, form **Questions** as to what the chapter will be about, **Read** the chapter, **Recite** the answers in your own words, and **Review** the answers several times). This technique serves to facilitate comprehension of what can be difficult textbook material and gives students a purpose for reading.

**WHO:**          Middle Grades, High School

**WHEN:**        During a lesson

**THEME(S):**   All

- Posters are an interesting way to study events or periods in history since effective posters use symbols that are unusual, simple, and direct. A great source for posters can be found at the *National Archives* or the *Library of Congress*. Select a poster from the time period or event you are studying, such as *Rosie the Riveter*. Help students see the impact of the poster by having them make the following observations:

    o What are the main colors used?
    o What symbols, if any, are used?
    o Are the symbols clear, memorable, and/or dramatic?
    o What is the message in the poster?
    o Who created the poster? (government, special interest groups, a for-profit company, and so forth)
    o Who is the intended audience for the poster?
    o What response was the creator of the poster hoping to achieve?
    o What purpose does the poster serve? Students can then make their own posters using the aforementioned criteria.

**WHO:**          Middle Grades, High School

**WHEN:**        During a lesson

**THEME(S):**   All

- When lecturing, PowerPoint can be a wonderful visual tool but it is overused. Try to keep any PowerPoint presentation in line with the average attention span of your students, such as 12 minutes for a 12-year-old or 17 minutes for a 17-year-old. However, stop periodically between slides and intersperse activity. Have your students do something with the information in the PowerPoint, such as talk with their partner or keep an appointment. Have a miniature copy of your presentation for your students since they will want to take notes from it rather than listening to you. Be sure your visuals and your voice go together.

**WHO:**        High School

**WHEN:**      During a lesson

**THEME(S):**    People, Places, and Environments

- Have students select a natural disaster, such as Hurricane Katrina, the tsunamis in Indonesia or Japan, or the earthquake in Christ Church, New Zealand. Have them create a visual depicting the immediate and long-range impact on the land and the people living in the areas affected (National Council for the Social Studies, 2010).

**WHO:**        Early and Middle Grades, High School

**WHEN:**      Before and during a lesson

**THEME(S):**    Culture; People, Places, and Environments; Individual Development and Identity

- Send a letter home to families asking them to send an appropriate photo of a student engaged in an activity with other family members or friends. This photo will be used in a social studies activity. If there are students who do not have access to such photos, then take a picture of those students engaged in activities with other students around campus. Make color copies of the photos and record each student's name on the back of the picture. Multiple photos can fit on one color page. Discuss with students the work of the social scientist and the role that photographs can play as primary sources. Start the discussion by showing a personal photo of you with family or friends and having them discuss what the photo tells about your life. Then divide the class into pairs and have each student exchange their photo with their partner. Have students record their thoughts in writing on what is happening in the picture of their partner. Some of the following questions could be recorded on the board to guide students' thinking:

  o Who is in the picture?
  o How are the people in the picture connected?
  o Can you decide where and when the photo was taken?
  o Are there objects that tell you about the people?

Have them share their thoughts with their partner, who can then confirm or dispute the inferences made by the student. A whole-class discussion can ensue regarding what things a social scientist can discern from a photo and which things would be impossible to know (Melber & Hunter, 2010).

**WHO:**       Middle Grades, High School

**WHEN:**      During a lesson

**THEME(S):**  People, Places, and Environments

- Have students use the visual of a world map to determine the distance and location of cities currently in the news. Have them answer the following questions orally or in writing by using current headlines:

  o Why are these cities in the news?
  o How long would it take to travel from city to city using a car, train, or plane?
  o If you were able to visit one place in the news, where would you go?
  o What problems might you encounter?
  o What places would you avoid? Why?
  o What is the climate like in the city you selected?

**WHO:**       High School

**WHEN:**      During and after a lesson

**THEME(S):**  Production, Distribution, and Consumption

- Have students work in cooperative groups to watch the trends in the stock market over a specified period of time, such as a week, a month, a quarter, or a semester. Have them look in the local newspaper or on the Internet in the *Market Watch* section for appropriate visuals. Have them research what each of the following indices shows: the *Dow Jones* industrial average, *the Nasdaq Composite,* and the *S&P 500*. Have students determine whether specific stocks are making or losing money from the charts and graphs shown and what political, social, and environmental factors may be influencing the growth of the stocks.

## REFLECTION AND APPLICATION

> How will I incorporate *visuals* into
> instruction to engage students' brains?

*Which visuals am I already incorporating into my social studies curriculum?*

*What additional visuals will I incorporate?*

# Strategy 19

# Work-Study and Apprenticeships

## WHAT: DEFINING THE STRATEGY

A learning style theorist, Robert Sternberg (2000), relates that much of what students learn in school does not prepare them for the professions that they will encounter in the real world. The U.S. Secretary's Commission on the Acquisition of Necessary Skills (SCANS; 1991) reports eight categories of competencies essential for success in the workplace. These include *interpersonal skills, problem solving, technology, information,* and *allocation of resources.* If a teacher incorporates the 20 brain-compatible strategies found in this book into daily instruction, students are better prepared for success in school and the real world as well. Chapter 13: Reciprocal Teaching and Cooperative Learning will equip students with the social skills so needed for working with diverse groups of people. Chapter 16: Technology addresses the student's ability to use technology for locating information and problem solving. But this chapter is probably the best one in the book for assisting students in acquiring relevant information and knowing how to allocate the resources of people, time, space, and money in the workplace.

The strategy of work-study refers to apprenticeships and internships. It is learning to do a job while working with someone who is already in that job. In the medical profession, work-study would be a medical student's internship and residency. In the teaching profession, it is a prospective teacher's time spent with a supervising teacher serving as a student teacher. However, social studies is one of the best content areas for involving students in the strategy of work-study. By the time students have interned with local, state, and national politicians, run a school store to learn the principles of supply and demand, and implemented a service-learning project that improves conditions for people in the real world while mastering

**151**

curriculum objectives, social studies instruction becomes relevant and memorable. After all, brains were not originally created to make straight *As* in school or score high on a test such as the *SAT*. Brains were made for solving problems in the real world, which enables the body to survive.

## WHY: THEORETICAL FRAMEWORK

The five steps inherent in service/community learning are as follows: (1) Be certain that all stakeholders are involved in the project's development; (2) collaborate by gaining support and making partnerships; (3) integrate the service learning with academic content and skills; (4) serve the community by making it a better place to live; (5) reflect or relive the service to gain new understandings; and (6) celebrate the project's success and honor those who made the commitment to become involved (National Council for the Social Studies, 2010).

Participating in community organizations that work to address cultural, political, social, and religious beliefs and interests is a civic engagement strategy that prepares students to become responsible citizens (National Council for the Social Studies, 2010).

An authentic model of social studies accurately replicates the real-life process of social science research (Melber & Hunter, 2010).

When there is real-world application in the classroom, knowledge is connected to authentic situations that occur both inside and outside the classroom as well (Tileston, 2011).

When the learning is made applicable to students' lives and a variety of ways by which they can learn is provided, students become more engaged, are more responsible for completing assignments, and realize that success in school can be meaningful (Algozzine, Campbell, & Wang, 2009b).

When students are taught to connect new learning with their real world, that new learning becomes more relevant (Allen, 2008a).

When high school students are required to cover a large amount of content but never have the opportunity to use that content within the context of authentic situations, it can become very problematic (Wiggins & McTighe, 2008).

In order to make social studies content relevant to students' lives, economic ideas should be taught within the context of real-life situations (Parker, 2009).

There are large gaps between the type of performance required for success in a business setting and that which is required for success in the school setting. Therefore, schools are producing educated adults who are unable to do what is expected of them in the work setting (Sternberg & Grigorenko, 2000).

Service or community learning can assist students in making their communities a better place in which to live (Committee on Developments in the Science of Learning, 1999).

Students benefit from the generous and empathetic feelings they experience when involved in service learning, which integrates students' educational background with service (Witmer & Anderson, 1994).

# HOW: INSTRUCTIONAL ACTIVITIES

**WHO:**        Early Grades

**WHEN:**      After a lesson

**THEME(S):**   All

- Elementary teachers must think of ways for their students to become socially conscious or to become active participants in the real world. Service learning is one of the best methods for accomplishing this objective. Have students brainstorm ways that they can be of service in their school and/or community. For example, they could collect clothing and food for needy families in the community. Have them select one or two projects that they can actually do. Have them work together to plan and implement the project. See how many social studies curricular objectives can be integrated into this service-learning project. The steps for implementing a service-learning project are in the first piece of research in this chapter.

**WHO:**        Early Grades

**WHEN:**      During a lesson

**THEME(S):**   All

- Work-study is typically found more often at the middle and high school grades; however, elementary students can become involved in service learning as well. For example, have students grow lavender in a community garden, make sachet packets, and donate them to a local retirement home.

**WHO:**        Early and Middle Grades, High School

**WHEN:**      Before a lesson

**THEME(S):**   Production, Distribution, and Consumption

- Have students adopt several local businesses and track their success or lack of it over a specified period of time. If the school is adopted by a business, that business may be willing to become involved in this project. Have students interview employees of the business in an effort to ascertain information about what product or service the business provides, what the demand is for that product, how they supply the product, and basically the current state of the business. Use real-life examples from the business as you teach concepts of production, distribution, and consumption so that students can link these concepts to the real world.

**WHO:**      Middle Grades, High School

**WHEN:**     After a lesson

**THEME(S):**  Global Connections

- Have students work individually or in cooperative groups to select a local business or public agency and then research the business, including interviewing employees to determine what global connections the business has and how those connections affect operations in the United States. Have students present this information to the class in a format of their choosing including PowerPoint, a written report, a news broadcast, and so forth.

**WHO:**      Middle Grades, High School

**WHEN:**     After a lesson

**THEME(S):**  All

- Teachers of middle and high school students can arrange in advance for their class members to be of service to the community. Service projects could include planning and growing a garden, which helps to feed people in the community; helping victims of tornadoes, floods, or fires to acquire their basic needs; or uniting with an ecological organization to study streams or eliminate pollution.

**WHO:**      High School

**WHEN:**     After a lesson

**THEME(S):**  Production, Distribution, and Consumption

- A wonderful project in which students can become involved would be *Habitat for Humanity*, which can be found in every state in the United States. Have the class research the concept and find the purpose for this service organization, including how one qualifies to have a house built and how one becomes involved in building one. Then have students volunteer to participate in the building of a house in their community, if the opportunity presents itself. Have them keep a journal of the experience from beginning to end.

**WHO:**      Early and Middle Grades, High School

**WHEN:**     After a lesson

**THEME(S):**  All

- Consult or have students consult the Web site www.servicelearning .com to ascertain ways to make service learning an integral part of the social studies curriculum.

**WHO:**       High School

**WHEN:**      After a lesson

**THEME(S):**  Power, Authority, and Governance

- Prior to local, state, or national elections, have students work as interns in support of a politician. Have them study the position for which the candidate is running and find out what the responsibilities and duties of that position are. Have students then research the platform of each politician and make personal decisions on which candidate they wish to support. Then have them contact the candidate's local office to find ways in which they can get involved in the campaign. Have them keep a log of the tasks performed and the number of hours spent working for the campaign. Following the internship, students can write about their real-life experience in this relevant application of social studies content.

**WHO:**       Early and Middle Grades, High School

**WHEN:**      Before a lesson

**THEME(S):**  Production, Distribution, and Consumption

- Under a teacher's direction, have students plan for, open, and operate a school store from which students in the entire school can buy supplies that will be needed during the school day. Students can determine which items will be sold in the store, from where they will be bought, and for what price they will be sold. Students can take turns apprenticing in the school store while mastering the real-life concept of supply and demand. Have the entire class follow the progress of the store's business and use it as an example when teaching economic concepts in class.

**WHO:**       Early and Middle Grades, High School

**WHEN:**      After a lesson

**THEME(S):**  All

- Invite professionals in the community whose real-life professions relate to a social studies objective you are teaching to come to your classroom to share the day-to-day responsibilities of their position with your students. Have students research the profession and prepare questions ahead of time to ask of the speaker. Assist students in ascertaining what is needed to prepare themselves for a similar position, such as what personal qualities and level of education are needed.

## REFLECTION AND APPLICATION

> How will I incorporate *work-study and apprenticeships* into instruction to engage students' brains?

**Which work-study and apprenticeship activities am I already incorporating into my social studies curriculum?**

**What additional activities will I incorporate?**

# Strategy 20

# Writing and Journals

## WHAT: DEFINING THE STRATEGY

Writing is cross-curricular and should be an integral part of the teaching of any content area. Social studies is not an exception. Writing should not be viewed as a separate subject, but students should be provided with real-life reasons to write, which include the following: to persuade, to inform, or to entertain. Here is an example of an activity that involves students in writing for the purpose of persuading others to concur with their point of view.

Explain to students that many new laws are passed at different levels of government each year. Yet, it is possible for a bill that a government official sponsored to not pass and, therefore, not become a law. Have students think about life in their communities, states, and nation. Have them think of any changes that they would like to see happen through the passage of new laws. Have students identify two new laws that they would like to see passed and write an editorial about the proposed laws. The editorial should be as persuasive as possible regarding the justification for the new legislation. Since teachers should always provide exemplars, or excellent examples, of the type of writing that is required, you may want to select sample well-written editorials from the newspaper prior to beginning this activity so that students have a feel for this type of writing. The class could also work together to develop a scoring rubric for assessing the editorials of all students in the class.

Writing not only organizes information in the brain; the brain tends to remember what the hand writes down. For this reason, students in your social studies classroom should be naturally engaged in brief, as well as in-depth, opportunities to write. In the middle of a lesson, stop and engage students in *quick writes*. Have them take 1 or 2 minutes to write down something you want to be sure that they recall. Here are a few examples of social studies *quick writes*. *Write two causes of the Civil War. Write the names of the original 13 colonies. Write the three branches of the federal government.* Have students write, write, and then write some more!

## WHY: THEORETICAL FRAMEWORK

When students make entries into learning journals, they are able to summarize the learning, recount their individual successes, and set short- and long-term goals (Gregory & Herndon, 2010).

Summarizing and note-taking are two research-based literacy strategies that should be used after reading (National Council for the Social Studies, 2010).

Students should develop a writing vocabulary, spell correctly, learn to organize text, think in hierarchies, and write in a number of different genres (Fogarty, 2009).

When students create and score their own scoring rubrics, they experience a sense of control over their writing, they learn to evaluate their work critically, and their writing is more guided and focused (Algozzine, Campbell, & Wang, 2009b).

Quick writes help teachers evaluate whether students' responses are accurate and assist them in clearing up misunderstandings (Jensen & Nickelsen, 2008).

Students need to be able to write in a variety of formats and structures, including short notes, business letters, expository essays, and creative fiction (Fogarty, 2009).

Journals and guiding questions focus students' attention on the topic, provide another tool for monitoring how well they have understood the content, and allow students to freely express their ideas without fear of being ostracized (Algozzine, Campbell, & Wang, 2009b).

Students should write about how the content they are learning has application for their personal lives (Jensen, 2008).

A neurotransmitter that aids the brain in forming long-term memories called acetylcholine is released when neurons connect through speech and through writing (Hannaford, 2005).

Written correspondence such as postcards and letters can give students insights into the past in a relevant way and can help them understand a historical event through first-person narrative (McCormick, 2004).

# HOW: INSTRUCTIONAL ACTIVITIES

**WHO:**         Middle Grades, High School

**WHEN:**        During a lesson

**THEME(S):**    All

- Talk to students prior to asking them to write during a social studies lecture. If you show visuals, such as PowerPoint, while you are talking, students will begin to take notes rather than listening to you (Karten, 2009).

**WHO:**         Early and Middle Grades

**WHEN:**        During a lesson

**THEME(S):**    Time, Continuity, and Change

- To understand the concept of how events change over time, have students construct a written time line of the most important events in their own personal lives from birth to their current age. Have them share their time lines with the entire class and use these as an introduction to how the lives of people in the present differ from the lives of those living in the past.

**WHO:**         Early and Middle Grades, High School

**WHEN:**        During a lesson

**THEME(S):**    Time, Continuity, and Change

- Following a specific lesson on life in the past, have students visualize that they lived in that period and write stories describing what their lives would have been like from a first-person perspective. Have them employ all of their senses and describe in writing what they would have seen, smelled, tasted, touched, and heard in their past life.

**WHO:**         Middle Grades, High School

**WHEN:**        During a lesson

**THEME(S):**    People, Places, and Environments; Individual Development and Identity

- Assign a significant historical figure to each student or have him or her select one. Have students complete the following *History Bio Poem* regarding that person:

  Line 1:  *Historical figure's first name?*
  Line 2:  *Lived in?* (what time frame)
  Line 3:  *Lived in?* (what locations)
  Line 4:  *Personal traits?* (two or three words that describe the person)

Line 5:   *Who loved?* (two or three things, people, or ideas the person loved)

Line 6:   *Who experienced?* (two or three feelings the person experienced)

Line 7:   *Who wanted?* (two or three things the person wanted to see happen)

Line 8:   *Who said?* (a direct quote from the person)

Line 9:   *What accomplished?* (a line explaining the person's importance or accomplishments)

Line 10: *Historical figure's last name?*

**WHO:**         Middle Grades, High School

**WHEN:**       After a lesson

**THEME(S):**    All

- Have students write an original editorial to a local paper taking a particular stance on an important issue of historical significance. Have them cite evidence from history in support of their position (National Council for the Social Studies, 2010).

**WHO:**         Middle Grades, High School

**WHEN:**       After a lesson

**THEME(S):**    Individual Development and Identity

- Have students visualize their lives 5 or 10 years into the future. In a personal journal, have them write down some short- and long-range goals that can assist them in achieving the future that they have envisioned. Have them put in writing the action steps they would need to take to accomplish the goals that they have delineated. For example, I knew that I wanted to be a teacher when I was 6 years old and by age 8, I had already made a plan to become one. The rest is history!

**WHO:**         Early and Middle Grades, High School

**WHEN:**       After a lesson

**THEME(S):**    All

- Integrate writing with graphic organizers by using the following activity. Have students create a graphic organizer for a historical event by folding a piece of paper and then unfolding it to create four squares. See the diagram below.

On page 1, which is the top left-hand side of the paper, have students respond to the following in writing:

   ○ One detailed sentence about the (historical event).
   ○ Another detailed sentence about the (historical event).

o A third detailed sentence about the (historical event).

o The most important thing I learned about the (historical event).

On page 2, which is the top right-hand side of the paper, have students draw a symbol to represent what they have learned. On page 3, which is the bottom left-hand side of the paper, have students write any questions that they still have. On page 4, which is the bottom right-hand side of the paper, have students respond to the following prompt: I feel _____ about the (historical event) because _____.

| | |
|---|---|
| The most important thing:<br><br><br><br>Page 1 | Symbol to represent<br>what I have learned:<br><br><br>Page 2 |
| Questions I still have:<br><br><br><br>Page 3 | I feel _____ about<br>the (historical event)<br>because _____.<br><br>Page 4 |

**WHO:**        Middle Grades, High School

**WHEN:**       After a lesson

**THEME(S):**    Civic Ideals and Practices

- Have students select an important civic issue and, after consulting a variety of sources, write a position paper taking a personal stance on the issue. The position they take should be substantiated by multiple sources and written up and presented to the class in a persuasive and convincing way.

**WHO:**        Middle Grades, High School

**WHEN:**       After a lesson

**THEME(S):**    All

- When students have taken notes following a lecture or after having read a section of text, have them share their notes with a peer. As they discuss the content, have them look for similarities and differences in the notes and add any pertinent information to their notes from their partner's that may have been omitted.

**WHO:**         Middle Grades, High School

**WHEN:**        During or after a lesson

**THEME(S):**    All

- When note-taking, have students take *Double-Column Notes*, similar to the visual below, which enable students to write the information in one column and encode it in the second column in a number of different ways, such as with graphic organizers or drawings.

## Double-Column Notes

| Drawings, Graphic Organizers, Charts, Graphs | Notes, Phrases, Information |
|---|---|
| Summary | |

(Feinstein, 2009)

**WHO:**         Elementary and Middle Grades, High School

**WHEN:**        After a lesson

**THEME(S):**    All

- Give each student a colored 3-by-5 card. Following a social studies lesson just taught, have students write down as much as they can remember about the lesson. Allow students to use these cards during a subsequent exam. This enables students to highlight the key points of the lesson and provides a written review of the information (Gregory & Herndon, 2010).

**WHO:**         Elementary and Middle Grades, High School

**WHEN:**        During or after a lesson

**THEME(S):**    All

- When a social studies report or research or theme paper is assigned, all students, but particularly those with learning disabilities, can use the mnemonic device *SCORE A* to remember the following effective writing strategy:

**S** Select a subject

**C** Create categories

**O** Obtain resources

**R** Read and take notes

**E** Evenly organize the information

**A** Apply the process writing steps

Planning

Drafting

Revising

(Bender, 2008, p. 93)

**WHO:**          Middle Grades, High School

**WHEN:**        During a lesson

**THEME(S):**    People, Places, and Environments

- Explain to students that many of the stories they read in their local newspaper are about people and locations far away, which makes it difficult to identify with the topic. Tell them that good writers and editors are able to *make a story hit home* by letting the reader know why they should care about a particular story, such as a drought or an earthquake halfway around the world. Have students select a newspaper story or one from the Internet where the location is outside of the United States. After reading the story, have them write several paragraphs regarding how the events in the story affect them either directly or indirectly. They should *make their story hit home.*

**WHO:**          High School

**WHEN:**        During a lesson

**THEME(S):**    All

- Have students take the point of view of an individual in history, such as a U.S. soldier who has just reached a concentration camp in Germany during World War II. Have them write a letter or postcard home to their family describing what they see and how they feel in vivid detail.

**WHO:**          Middle Grades, High School

**WHEN:**        During a lesson

**THEME(S):**    People, Places, and Environments

- At the culmination of specific social studies units, have students express their opinion of the unit in writing in their personal journals. They could answer the following questions:

  o What did you like best about this unit?
  o What did you like least about this unit?
  o What were your favorite (least favorite) teaching strategies used during this unit?
  o If this unit were to be taught again, what activities would you change?

# REFLECTION AND APPLICATION

How will I incorporate *writing and journals* into instruction to engage students' brains?

*Which writing and journal activities am I already incorporating into my social studies curriculum?*

*What additional activities will I incorporate?*

# Resource

*Brain-Compatible Lesson Design*

**B**y now, the dendrites should be growing in your own brain. You should be reflecting on which activities in this book are appropriate for your students if you use them just as they are, which activities can be adapted, and which new activities can be created using the 20 brain-compatible strategies. Let me offer some help to you. I have developed a lesson plan that will assist you in developing memorable lessons that not only incorporate the strategies but also capture and keep the attention of your students. A brain-compatible social studies sample lesson plan can be found at the end of the chapter. Each of the major sections of this plan is described in the paragraphs that follow. It is not necessary that you write or type your plan on the form itself. What is essential is that you are able to ask and answer the following five questions every time you plan a lesson if you want to ensure that the lesson is brain-compatible.

## SECTION 1: LESSON OBJECTIVE ■

### What will you be teaching?

The obvious first question when planning a brain-compatible lesson is to consider what you are getting ready to teach. This question is not yours to answer. It is determined by your social studies themes and the objectives that naturally flow from those themes. If you attempt to let your textbook determine what you will be teaching, you may not be addressing the knowledge, skills, behaviors, or attitudes that are expected for your grade level or content area. Your social studies book is only one resource for addressing that knowledge and may not even be the best resource. In addition, if you are only using the textbook, you may feel overwhelmed that you will never cover all of the content. You shouldn't!

A concern that I share with teachers throughout the United States as I present is their concern about the overwhelming number of objectives that teachers are expected to teach and students to master. Consider this. The textbooks in many school systems around the world are one-third the size of textbooks in the United States, and yet many countries outscore our students on tests of academic achievement. Could it be that less is more? Could it be that teachers should examine their curriculum and identify those major concepts that every student needs to know? Could it be that some of those concepts could be chunked or connected together and taught simultaneously? The good news is that the National Council for the Social Studies has already identified those chunks and called them themes. Continue to examine your curriculum for those concepts that should be taught together so that students can more easily see the connections in the content.

In our opening scenarios, both teachers were addressing the *Power, Authority, and Governance* theme with specific emphasis on the *Declaration of Independence.* Now that we know what we are teaching, the remainder of this lesson plan will reflect on how Mr. Martinez made it a brain-compatible, unforgettable lesson for students while Mrs. Simpson did not. The objective is for students to comprehend the purpose and major tenets of *The Unanimous Declaration of the Thirteen United States of America.*

## ■ SECTION 2: ASSESSMENT

### How will you know students have learned the content?

Waiting until you plan your lesson and then deciding what your students should know and be able to do at the end of it is actually too late. The research on assessment says, as soon as you know what you will be teaching, the next question becomes, how will I know students have learned the content I am teaching?

When I was a student in school, we spent our time trying to guess what the teacher was going to put on the test. If we guessed correctly, we made an *A.* However, we may have guessed incorrectly, and still failed, even though we studied. We just studied the wrong thing! Determine what knowledge, skills, behaviors, or attitudes you desire students to have by the end of the lesson and, by all means, tell them! Assessment should not be a well-kept secret. If student brains know what you expect, they stand a better chance of meeting your expectations. Here's an analogy. If you are an airplane pilot of a private plane, how can you plot your route before you know your destination? You can't! You also should not plan your lesson before you know your *destination* with students. That is why the assessment question is the second question of the five and not the fifth and last question.

In our sample lesson, students are told at the beginning that by the time they finish the lesson, they should be able to describe in writing from a personal point of view the purpose of the *Declaration of Independence* and its major tenets.

# SECTION 3: WAYS TO GAIN ■ AND MAINTAIN ATTENTION

## How will you gain and maintain students' attention?

### (Consider need, novelty, meaning, and emotion.)

I have good news and bad news. The good news is that there is so much stimuli in today's environment that the human brain cannot pay attention to everything at once. Therefore, people can be very selective about what they choose to pay attention to. If a teacher's lesson is not worthy of attention, then students' attention is going elsewhere. When the lesson is boring, students are conversing with their peers, peering out the window, text messaging while holding the phone under their desktop, paying attention to who is going down the hall, or simply daydreaming. Students can even maintain eye contact with you and not pay a bit of attention to your lesson.

Here's another bit of bad news: There is a structure in the brain called the hippocampus that helps to determine which parts of what you learn will end up in long-term memory. If your lesson is not deemed important, it stands little chance of getting past the hippocampus. In fact, the hippocampus will hit the delete key at night and your lesson will figuratively end up in the *trash*. How can you tell if your lesson was deleted? When they come back to class 24 hours later, it is as if students were not present when you were teaching the initial lesson. Has that ever happened to you? It certainly has to me!

The good news is if you want to grab students' attention, hold it throughout your lesson, and keep your lesson out of the *trash*, there are four ways to do it. They are **need, novelty, meaning**, and **emotion.**

*Need*

Have you ever learned or remembered something simply because you needed to know it? I have. I did not see the need to memorize the telephone numbers of my three children since they were all programmed into my cell phone. Therefore, no matter where I was in the world, I could push a button on my phone and their voices would be at the other end. Then one day, while I was out of the country, my cell phone died. I could not retrieve their numbers from the phone nor had I ever written their numbers down or memorized them, and I desperately needed to talk to my daughter Jennifer, who was pregnant at the time. I now have my children's numbers stored in my head. I have seen the need to memorize them so that this will not happen to me again! Mr. Martinez led students in a whole-class discussion of the rationale for celebrating July 4 in the United States and what that means to our freedom.

Sometimes *need* will not work with students. After all, you know that they need specific knowledge or a certain skill, but they do not perceive the same need. In fact, just telling them that they will need to know the information for a standardized or teacher-made test is not enough to inspire most students. The good news is that you have three other ways to gain their attention. The second one is *Novelty*.

## Novelty

Have you ever noticed that the brain pays attention to things that are new or different in the environment? Things to which we are accustomed become mundane and require little special attention. If students can expect that every day in your social studies class, the teaching activities, such as lecture or worksheets, will be the same, they are soon paying very little attention to what you are asking them to do. As the content changes, so should the strategies.

You may be saying, *But, there are only 20 strategies on the entire list. Where is the novelty in that?* Well, think about it. Every one of those 20 strategies has inherent in it endless possibilities for novelty. Think of all of the different stories you can tell, the music you can incorporate, or even the social studies role plays or projects in which you can engage your students. The possibilities are endless!

In the sample lesson, Mr. Martinez uses a number of the 20 strategies at some point during the lesson to teach students about the *Declaration of Independence*. Those strategies will be delineated as we answer question five.

## Meaning

Students have often been heard asking this question: *Why do we have to learn this?* This question indicates that students see no relevance in what is being taught and how it applies to their personal lives. For content to be meaningful, it needs to be connected in some way to students' lives in the real world. After all, the true purpose of the brain is survival in the real world. Here is an example. I was observing in a classroom where a teacher was having a difficult time getting students to understand the concept of *propaganda*. They had talked about it, read about it, and looked it up in the dictionary. It was not until she put up a visual of the popular singer *Rihanna* that the concept hit home. In the visual, Rihanna is advertising eye makeup. The company of the makeup wants the public to believe that this makeup is superior simply because Rihanna is wearing it. However, there is no definitive proof that this makeup is better than any other. This whole scenario illustrates the concept of how advertisers use propaganda to influence the public. In the scenario, Mr. Martinez had students write their own declaration of independence from their parents, which makes the original document much more meaningful!

## Emotion

Of all four ways to gain the brain's attention, emotion is probably the most powerful. Why? Emotion places information in one of the strongest memory systems in the brain, reflexive memory. Anything that happened in the world that was emotional, you will not soon forget where you were when it happened. Let's try one. Do you remember where you were when you heard that the *Challenger* shuttle had exploded and the United States lost seven astronauts? If you were old enough, you probably will remember exactly where you were and what you were doing even though that happened more than 25 years ago!

Yet, teachers do not want to engage students in negative emotional experiences that are not good for learning. Although students will never forget the experience of being in a negative teacher's class, they will not remember the content acquired during the experience. For example, when I am reading on a plane, as long as the flight is smooth and there is light to moderate turbulence, I can concentrate on the text and comprehend what I am reading. However, several times I have been on flights where we encountered extreme turbulence. All of a sudden, even if I pretend to be calm and reading, I am reading the same paragraph over and over, and if questioned, I would not remember one thing that I am supposedly reading. The ride has become too emotional! My definition of an emotional teacher is one who teaches with enthusiasm and passion and gets students excited about learning. In the scenario, Mr. Martinez had students reflect on whether they would want to present their declaration to their parents. Students discussed emotionally how this might affect their relationship with people who love and care for them.

A teacher does not need to feel compelled to include all four ways to get a student's attention: need, novelty, meaning, and emotion. If he or she can effectively incorporate one, that one can lead to a great lesson.

## SECTION 4: CONTENT CHUNKS ■

### How will you divide and teach the content to engage students' brains?

Join me in an activity that will help to prove that the brain thinks in connections. Try this with students or even with members of your family. Ask them to spell the word shop three times. (s-h-o-p, s-h-o-p, s-h-o-p). Then quickly ask them, *What do you do when you get to a green light?* Nine times out of ten, the answer will be *stop*, when the correct answer is *go*. The brain connected or associated the word *light* with the rhyming word *shop*. The closest connection between those two words in many brains is the word *stop*.

When you think about connecting content together, remember that even the adult brain can only hold between five and nine, or an average of seven, isolated facts in short-term memory simultaneously. This is why so much in life comes in a series of sevens. For example, there are 7 days in a week, numbers in a phone number, notes on the scale, colors in the rainbow, seas, continents, habits of highly effective people, initial multiple intelligences, or even dwarfs.

If we are expected to hold more than seven items, then the content needs to be chunked, or connected. This is why the social security number, a telephone number, or a credit card number is in chunks—to make it easier to remember. The brain considers a chunk as one thing, rather than separate things. Therefore, look at your curriculum and identify those major chunks under each theme that every student needs to know in social studies during the school year. For example, when you study immigration, address the various groups who have immigrated throughout history, not just one group.

Remember to include at least one activity in each chunk you teach. This activity gives the brain time and energy for processing the chunk. Your students will thank you for it!

In the sample lesson, Mr. Martinez opened class with a review activity during which students were reviewing vocabulary words. He then needed only one chunk (or lesson segment) to teach the *Declaration of Independence*. However, he engaged students in a number of different activities within that one lesson segment to capture students' brains.

## ■ SECTION 5: BRAIN-COMPATIBLE STRATEGIES

### Which will you use to deliver content?

All 20 of the brain-compatible strategies are listed at the bottom of the lesson plan. In this way, teachers will not have to remember them because they will have them listed for ready reference. Even I can't always remember the 20 strategies when I need to do so and I wrote the book! As you are determining what activities you will include in each chunk of your lesson, you should be incorporating some of the 20 brain-compatible strategies. If you get to the end of your plan and you cannot check off any of the strategies (possibly because your entire lesson consisted of long lectures or worksheets, neither of which is brain-compatible), go back and plan your lesson again! It is not brain-compatible and will not meet the needs of the majority of your students. Much of it may not even be recalled after a 24-hour period.

I have often been asked this question: *How many strategies should I incorporate in one lesson, or one chunk?* There is no magic number. Using too many strategies at one time can be just as detrimental as using too few. A rule of thumb I try to teach by is as follows: Make sure that at some point during the lesson you have incorporated at least one visual, one auditory, one tactile, and one kinesthetic strategy since you will have students with all four modality preferences in your classroom. That doesn't mean one strategy of each modality per chunk, but one strategy of each modality per objective.

Keep this in mind. If you use one strategy, say music, to teach a lesson, and the entire class grasps the concept, then by all means, move on to the next concept. You taught it and they got it! However, if you use one strategy, say music, to teach a lesson and part of the class understands the concept and the other part does not, use a different strategy from a different modality for the re-teaching. This is how you can best differentiate instruction. Simply doing the same thing again and louder has never worked!

By the time the lesson in our good scenario was completed, students had experienced at least eight of the 20 strategies: they had entered the classroom to patriotic *music* to set the mood for the day; they reviewed vocabulary using either *drawing* or *role play* while working with a partner (*reciprocal teaching*); they engaged in a whole-class *discussion* of the meaning of *The Unanimous Declaration of the Thirteen United States of America*; they read parts of it aloud while standing (*movement*); they wrote their own declaration (*writing*); and their personal declaration had to be analogous to the original document (*metaphor, analogy, and simile*).

## SUMMARY ■

Well, we've come to the end of another book. My hope is that I have accomplished what I set out to do, which was as follows:

1. Introduce you to 20 strategies that take advantage of ways in which the brain learns best;

2. Supply more than 200 research rationales from experts in the field as to why these strategies work better than others;

3. Provide more than 200 activities you can use to incorporate the 20 strategies into a K–12 social studies classroom;

4. Correlate the social studies content themes to each activity;

5. Allow time and space at the end of each chapter for the reader to reflect on the application of the strategies as they apply directly to the reader's specific objectives; and

6. Ask and answer the five questions that every teacher ought to be asking when planning and teaching a brain-compatible social studies lesson.

Of all the content areas, if not taught properly, social studies can become extremely boring as it was for me when I was in school. However, if taught in brain-compatible ways, it has the capability of being one of the most memorable and relevant content areas for any student. Take those major social studies concepts, or chunks, you will be teaching this year and incorporate these strategies not only to increase student achievement, but to get students so turned on to social studies that many may decide to become politicians, ethnographers, historians, or economists! At the very least, they will remember being in your class and the information necessary for becoming a more responsible citizen in a democratic society.

# BRAIN-COMPATIBLE SOCIAL STUDIES LESSON PLAN

**Lesson Objective(s):** *What will you be teaching?*

_____

**Assessment (Traditional/Authentic):** *How will you know students have learned the content?*

_____

**Ways to Gain/Maintain Attention (Primacy):** *How will you gain and maintain students' attention? Consider need, novelty, meaning, or emotion.*

_____

**Content Chunks:** *How will you divide and teach the content to engage students' brains?*

**Lesson Segment 1:**

**Activities:**

**Lesson Segment 2:**

**Activities:**

**Lesson Segment 3:**

**Activities:**

_____

**Brain-Compatible Strategies:** Which will you use to deliver content?

- ☐ Brainstorming/Discussion
- ☐ Drawing/Artwork
- ☐ Field Trips
- ☐ Games
- ☐ Graphic Organizers/Semantic Maps/Word Webs
- ☐ Humor
- ☐ Manipulatives/Experiments/ Labs/Models
- ☐ Metaphors/Analogies/ Similes
- ☐ Mnemonic Devices
- ☐ Movement
- ☐ Music/Rhythm/Rhyme/Rap

- ☐ Project-/Problem-Based Instruction
- ☐ Reciprocal Teaching/ Cooperative Learning
- ☐ Role Plays/Drama/ Pantomimes/Charades
- ☐ Storytelling
- ☐ Technology
- ☐ Visualization/Guided Imagery
- ☐ Visuals
- ☐ Work-Study/ Apprenticeships
- ☐ Writing/Journals

# Bibliography

Adams, J. (2009). *The impact of kinesthetic activities on eighth grade benchmark scores* (Unpublished master's thesis). Gratz College: Melrose Park, PA.

Algozzine, B., Campbell, P., & Wang, A. (2009a). *63 tactics for teaching diverse learners: Grades K–6.* Thousand Oaks, CA: Corwin.

Algozzine, B., Campbell, P., & Wang, A. (2009b). *63 tactics for teaching diverse learners: Grades 6–12.* Thousand Oaks, CA: Corwin.

Allen, R. (2008a). *Green light classrooms: Teaching techniques that accelerate learning.* Victoria, Australia: Hawker Brownlow.

Allen, R. (2008b). *The ultimate book of music for learning.* Victoria, Australia: Hawker Brownlow.

Anderson, L. W., & Krathwohl, D. R. (2001). *A taxonomy for learning, teaching, and assessing.* New York: Addison Wesley Longman.

Baumgarten, S. (2006). Meaningful movement for children: Stay true to their natures. *Teaching Elementary Physical Education,* July, 9–11.

Bender, W. N. (2008). *Differentiating instruction for students with learning disabilities: Best teaching practices for general and special educators* (2nd ed.). Thousand Oaks, CA: Corwin & Council for Exceptional Children.

Berman, S. (2008). *Thinking strategies for science: Grades 5–12* (2nd ed.). Victoria, Australia: Hawker Brownlow.

Bloom, B. S. (Ed.). (1956). *Taxonomy of educational objectives: The classification of educational goals, by a committee of college and university examiners.* New York: Longmans.

Brand, S. T. (2006). Facilitating emergent literacy skills: A literature-based, multiple intelligence approach. *Journal of Research in Childhood Education, 21*(2), 133–148.

Burton, J. B., & McFarland, A. L. (2009). Multicultural resources. *General Music Today, 22*(2), 30–33.

Caine, R. N., Caine, G., McClintic, C., & Klimek, K. J. (2009). *12 brain/mind learning principles in action: Developing executive functions of the human brain* (2nd ed.). Thousand Oaks, CA: Corwin.

Calderon, M. (2007). *Teaching reading to English language learners, Grades 6–12.* Thousand Oaks, CA: Corwin.

Canestrari, A. (2005). Social studies and geography: Beyond rote memorization. In R. H. Auder & L. K. Jordan (Eds.), *Integrating inquiry across the curriculum* (pp. 17–42). Thousand Oaks, CA: Corwin.

Carney, R. N., & Levin, J. R. (2000). Mnemonic instruction, with a focus on transfer. *Journal of Educational Psychology, 92*(4), 783–790.

Chapin, J. R. (2005). *Elementary social studies: A practical guide.* Boston: Allyn & Bacon.

Committee on Developments in the Science of Learning. (1999). *How people learn: Brain, mind, experience, and school* (J. D. Bransford, A. L. Brown, & R. R. Cockney, Eds.). Washington, DC: National Academies Press.

Costa, A. L. (2008). *School as a home for the mind: Creating mindful curriculum, instruction, and dialogue.* Victoria, Australia: Hawker Brownlow.

Costa-Giomi, E. (1998, April). *The McGill Piano Project: Effects of three years of piano instruction on children's cognitive abilities, academic achievement, and self-esteem.* Paper presented at the meeting of the Music Educators National Conference, Phoenix, AZ.

Craig, S., Hull, K., Haggart, A. G., & Crowder, E. (2001). Storytelling: Addressing the literacy needs of diverse learners. *Teaching Exceptional Children, 33*(5), 46–52.

Delandtsheer, J. (2011). *Making all kids smarter: Strategies that help all students reach their highest potential.* Thousand Oaks, CA: Corwin.

Dewey, J. (1934). *Art as experience.* New York: Minton Balch.

Dewey, J. (1938). *Experience and education.* New York: Macmillian.

DiCecco, V. M., & Gleason, M. M. (2002). Using graphic organizers to attain relational knowledge from expository text. *Journal of Learning Disabilities, 35*(4), 306–320.

Drake, S. (1996). Guided imagery and education: Theory, practice, and experience. *Journal of Mental Imagery, 20,* 1–58.

Duncombe, S., & Heikkinen, M. H. (1990). Role playing for different viewpoints. *Social Studies, 81*(1), 33–35.

Ekwall, E. E., & Shanker, J. L. (1988). *Diagnosis and remediation of the disabled reader* (3rd ed.). Boston: Allyn & Bacon.

Feinstein, S. G. (2009). *Secrets of the teenage brain: Research-based strategies for reaching and teaching today's adolescents* (2nd ed.). Thousand Oaks, CA: Corwin.

Fernandez, A. (Interviewer), & Klingberg, T. (Interviewee). (2006). *Working memory training and RoboMemo: Interview with Dr. Torkel Klingberg.* Retrieved from http://www.sharpbrains.com/blog/2006/09/25/working-memory-training-and-robomemo-interview-with-dr-torkel-klingberg

Fogarty, R. (2009). *Brain-compatible classrooms* (3rd ed.). Victoria, Australia: Hawker Brownlow.

Gardner, H. (1983). *Frames of mind: The theory of multiple intelligences.* New York: Basic Books.

Gettinger, M., & Kohler, K. M. (2006). Proces-outcome approaches to classroom management and effective teaching. In C. Evertson, C. M. Weinstein, & C. S. Weinstein (Eds.), *Handbook of classroom management: Research, practice, and contemporary issues* (pp. 73–95). Mahwah, NJ: Erlbaum.

Goodnough, K. (2006). Enhancing pedagogical content knowledge through self-study: An exploration of problem-based learning. *Teaching in Higher Education, 11,* 301–318.

Gregory, G. H., & Herndon, L. E. (2010). *Differentiated instructional strategies for the block schedule.* Thousand Oaks, CA: Corwin.

Gregory, G., & Parry, T. (2006). *Designing brain-compatible learning* (3rd ed.). Thousand Oaks, CA: Corwin.

Green, L. S., & Casale-Giannola, D. (2011). *40 active learning strategies for the inclusive classroom (Grades K–5).* Thousand Oaks, CA: Corwin.

Gullatt, D. E. (2008). Enhancing student learning through arts integration: Implications for the profession. *The High School Journal, 91*(4), 12–16.

Hannaford, C. (2005). *Smart moves* (2nd ed.). Salt Lake City, UT: Great Rivers Books.

Harada, V., & Kim, L. (2003). Problem-based instruction makes learning real. *Knowledge Quest, 32*(1), 33–34.

Hiraoka, L. (2006, March 13). All this talk about tech. *NEA Today, 24,* 6.

Hyerle, D. N., & Alper, L. (2011). Student successes with thinking maps. *School-based research, results, and models for achievement using visual tools* (2nd ed.). Thousand Oaks, CA: Corwin.

Janson, H. W., & Janson, A. F. (2003). *History of art* (6th ed., Rev.). Upper Saddle River, NJ: Pearson/Prentice Hall.

Jensen, E. (2001). *Arts with the brain in mind.* Alexandria, VA: Association for Supervision and Curriculum Development.

Jensen, E. (2002). *Learning with the body in mind.* Thousand Oaks, CA: Corwin.

Jensen, E. (2005). *Top tunes for teaching: 977 song titles and practical tools for choosing the right music every time.* Thousand Oaks, CA: Corwin.

Jensen, E. (2008). *Brain-based learning: The new paradigm of teaching* (2nd ed.). Thousand Oaks, CA: Corwin.

Jensen, E. (2009). *Super teaching* (4th ed.). Thousand Oaks, CA: Corwin.

Jensen, E., & Nickelsen, L. (2008). *Deeper learning: 7 powerful strategies for in-depth and longer-lasting learning.* Victoria, Australia: Hawker Brownlow.

Jensen, R. (2008). *Catalyst teaching: High-impact teaching techniques for the science classroom.* Victoria, Australia: Hawker Brownlow.

Johnson, D., & Johnson, R. (1994). *Leading the cooperative school.* Edina, MN: Interaction.

Karten, T. J. (2009). *Inclusion strategies that work for adolescent learners!* Thousand Oaks, CA: Corwin.

Keeley, P. (2008). *Science formative assessment: 75 practical strategies for linking assessment, instruction, and learning.* Thousand Oaks, CA: Corwin & National Science Teachers Association.

Kluball, J. L. (2000). The relationship of instrumental music instruction and academic achievement for the senior class of 2000 at Lee County High School (Doctoral dissertation, University of Sarasota, 2000). *Dissertation Abstracts International, 61*(11), 4320A.

Krepel, W. J., & Duvall, C. R. (1981). *Field trips: A guide for planning and conducting educational experiences.* Washington, DC: National Education Association.

Lakoff, G., & Johnson, M. (1980). *Metaphors we live by.* Chicago: University of Chicago Press.

Lengel, T., & Kuczala, M. (2010). *The kinesthetic classroom: Teaching and learning through movement.* Thousand Oaks, CA: Corwin and the Regional Training Center.

Markowitz, K., & Jensen, E. (2007). *The great memory book.* Victoria, Australia: Hawker Brownlow Education.

Marzano, R. J. (2007). *The art and science of teaching: A comprehensive framework for effective instruction.* Victoria, Australia: Hawker Brownlow Education.

McCormick, T. M. (2004). Letters from Trenton, 1776: Teaching with primary sources. *Social Studies and the Young Learner, 17*(2), 5–12.

McCormick Tribune Foundation. (2004). *What every child needs* [DVD]. Chicago: Chicago Production Center.

Melber, L. M., & Hunter, A. (2010). *Integrating language arts and social studies: 25 strategies for K–8 inquiry-based learning.* Thousand Oaks, CA: Sage.

National Council for the Social Studies. (2010). *National curriculum standards for social studies: A framework for teaching, learning, and assessment.* Silver Springs, MD: National Council for the Social Studies.

Nevills, P., & Wolfe, P. (2009). *Building the reading brain: PreK–3* (2nd ed.). Thousand Oaks, CA: Corwin.

Olson, J. K., Cox-Petersen, A. M., & McComas, W. F. (2001). The inclusion of informal environments in science teacher preparation. *Journal of Science Teacher Education, 12*(3), 155–173.

Parker, W. C. (2009). *Social studies in elementary education.* Upper Saddle River, NJ: Prentice Hall.

Perez, K. (2008). *More than 100 brain-friendly tools and strategies for literacy instruction.* Thousand Oaks, CA: Corwin.

Prensky, M. (2009, February). H. Sapiens Digital: From digital immigrants and digital natives to digital wisdom. *Innovate: Journal of Online Education, 5*(3).

Putman, E., & Rommel-Esham, K. (2004). Using oral history to study change: An integrated approach. *The Social Studies, 95*(5), 201–205.

Qais, F. (2007). Enlightening advantages of cooperative learning. ERIC online submission.

Ratey, J. (2008). *SPARK: The revolutionary new science of exercise and the brain.* New York: Little, Brown and Company.

Saenz, L. M., Fuchs, L. S., & Fuchs, D. (2005). Peer-assisted learning strategies for English language learners with learning disabilities. *Exceptional Children, 71*(3), 231–247.

Santrock, J. W. (2003). *Adolescence* (9th ed.). Boston: McGraw-Hill.

Sebesta, L. M., & Martin, S. R. M. (2004). Fractions: Building a foundation with concrete manipulatives. *Illinois Schools Journal, 83*(2), 3–23.

Secretary's Commission on Achieving Necessary Skills. (1991). *What work requires of schools: A SCANS report for America 2000.* Washington, DC: U.S. Department of Labor.

Selwyn, D. (1993). *Living history in the classroom: Integrative arts activities for making social studies meaningful.* Chicago: Zephyr.

Sheffield, C. (2007, summer). Technology and the gifted adolescent: Higher order thinking, 21st century literacy, and the Digital Native. *Meridan: A Middle School Computer Technologies Journal, 10*(2). Retrieved from http://www.ncsu.edu/meridian/sum2007

Sousa, D. A. (2006). *How the brain learns* (3rd ed.). Thousand Oaks, CA: Corwin.

Sousa, D. A. (2011). *How the ELL brain learns.* Thousand Oaks, CA: Corwin.

Sprenger, M. (2007). *Memory 101 for educators.* Thousand Oaks, CA: Corwin.

Sternberg, R. J., & Grigorenko, E. L. (2000). *Teaching for successful intelligence: To increase student learning and achievement.* Arlington Heights, IL: Skylight.

Summerford, C. (2000). *PE for me.* Champaign, IL: Human Kinetics.

Sunal, C. S., & Haas, M. E. (2005). *Social studies for the elementary and middle grades: A constructivist approach* (2nd ed.). Boston: Allyn & Bacon.

Sylwester, R. (2010). *A child's brain: The need for nuture.* Thousand Oaks, CA: Corwin.

Tanner, L. (2008). No child left behind is just the tip of the iceberg. *The Social Studies, 99*(1), 41–45.

Tate, M. L. (2007). *Shouting won't grow dendrites: 20 techniques for managing a brain-compatible classroom.* Thousand Oaks, CA: Corwin.

Tate, M. L. (2010). *Worksheets don't grow dendrites: 20 instructional strategies that engage the brain* (2nd ed.). Thousand Oaks, CA: Corwin.

Tate, M. L., & Phillips, W. G. (2011). *Science worksheets don't grow dendrites: 20 instructional strategies that engage the brain.* Thousand Oaks, CA: Corwin.

Tileston, D. W. (2011). *10 best teaching practices: How brain research and learning styles define teaching competencies* (3rd ed.). Thousand Oaks, CA: Corwin.

Udvari-Solner, A., & Kluth, P. (2008). *Joyful learning: Active and collaborative learning in inclusive classrooms.* Thousand Oaks, CA: Corwin.

Van Scotter, R., White, W. E., Hartoonian, H. M., & Davis, J. E. (2007). A gateway to social studies through topical history. *Social Studies, 98*(6), 231–235.

Walberg, H. J. (1999). Productive teaching. In H. C. Waxman & H. J. Walberg (Eds.), *New directions for teaching practice research* (pp. 75–104). Berkeley, CA: McCutchen.

Wang, A., & Thomas, M. (1995). Effects of keywords on long-term retention: Help or hindrance? *Journal of Educational Psychology, 87,* 468–475.

Wiggins, G., & McTighe, J. (2008, May). Put understanding first. *Educational Leadership, 65*(19), 36–41.

Witmer, J. T., & Anderson, C. S. (1994). *How to establish a high school service learning program.* Alexandria, VA: Association for Supervision and Curriculum Development.

Wolf, S. (2003). Teaching for critical literacy in social studies. *The Social Studies, 94*(3), 101–106.

# Index

# CORWIN

A SAGE Company

The Corwin logo—a raven striding across an open book—represents the union of courage and learning. Corwin is committed to improving education for all learners by publishing books and other professional development resources for those serving the field of PreK–12 education. By providing practical, hands-on materials, Corwin continues to carry out the promise of its motto: **"Helping Educators Do Their Work Better."**